colourful
fun
embroidery

**Featuring 24 modern projects to bring
joy and happiness to your life!**

I made this hoop for my beautiful girl, Evie, who inspires me every day. This book is for her. I love you so much, Little One.

For Evie

Dream big, Little One

colourful
fun
embroidery

**Featuring 24 modern projects to bring
joy and happiness to your life!**

CLARE ALBANS

*Photographs by Jesse Wild
and Clare Albans*

WHITE OWL

For Evie
Dream big, Little One

First published in Great Britain in 2020 by
PEN & SWORD WHITE OWL
An imprint of Pen & Sword Books Ltd
Yorkshire – Philadelphia

ISBN 9781526753854

Group Publisher: Jonathan Wright
Series Editor and Publishing Consultant: Katherine Raderecht
Art Director: Jane Toft
Editor: Katherine Raderecht
Photography: Jesse Wild and Clare Albans
Styling: Jaine Bevan
Models: Alice McDonald and Victoria Welsher

Printed and bound in India, by Replika Press Pvt. Ltd.

Pen & Sword Books Ltd incorporates the Imprints of Pen & Sword Books
Archaeology, Atlas, Aviation, Battleground, Discovery, Family History, History, Maritime,
Military, Naval, Politics, Railways, Select, Transport, True Crime, Fiction, Frontline Books,
Leo Cooper, Praetorian Press, Seaforth Publishing, Wharncliffe and White Owl.

For a complete list of Pen & Sword titles please contact:

PEN & SWORD BOOKS LIMITED
47 Church Street, Barnsley, South Yorkshire S70 2AS, England
E-mail: enquiries@pen-and-sword.co.uk
Website: www.pen-and-sword.co.uk
or
PEN AND SWORD BOOKS
1950 Lawrence Rd, Havertown, PA 19083, USA
E-mail: Uspen-and-sword@casematepublishers.com
Website: www.penandswordbooks.com

contents

introduction

I can't really imagine a day without doing something creative. Creativity has always been a big part of my life, whether I was practising the violin, trying out different crafts or learning to bake. However, only over the last year or so that I have come to realise just how important creativity is to me; not just because it is what I enjoy doing, but because when I am being creative, I am at my happiest. It is an integral part of me, of who I am and what I aspire to be. I really believe that being creative is being yourself. I love this quote from graphic artist, Anthony Burrill, which sums up my belief that doing something creative can have a really positive impact. Burrill says "you need to be yourself to be happy".

The subject of mindfulness has become very popular over the last couple of years and, increasingly, creativity is seen as going hand in hand with being mindful. According to mindful.org, the voice of the emerging mindfulness community, mindfulness is the 'ability to be fully present, aware of where we are and what we're doing, and not overly reactive or overwhelmed by what's going on around us'. Doing something creative allows us to really focus our energy on one specific activity and enjoy being in that moment, without worrying about anything else. Concentrating on a creative task like this helps you take time out, whether you consciously realise you are being mindful or not. You may not like the word 'mindfulness' or you might prefer to call it wellbeing or self care or even not give it a specific label at all – but do think about how you can use your creativity to help you to feel good.

When it comes to creativity, it is very common to be put off the idea of experimenting with new techniques or developing our ideas by a little voice in our head telling us that we won't be able to do it. This can sometimes mean we don't even start a creative project. Often we start a project, and then feel like it's going a bit wrong or it doesn't look as perfect as someone else's, so we give up on it. This is such a huge barrier to developing our creativity and wellbeing, but it can be overcome! I think creativity is an exploration of who we are and how we express ourselves, and a really important part of that process is learning to embrace making mistakes. This is one of the most important lessons I have learned over the past few years of creating and experimenting. If I'm in a place where

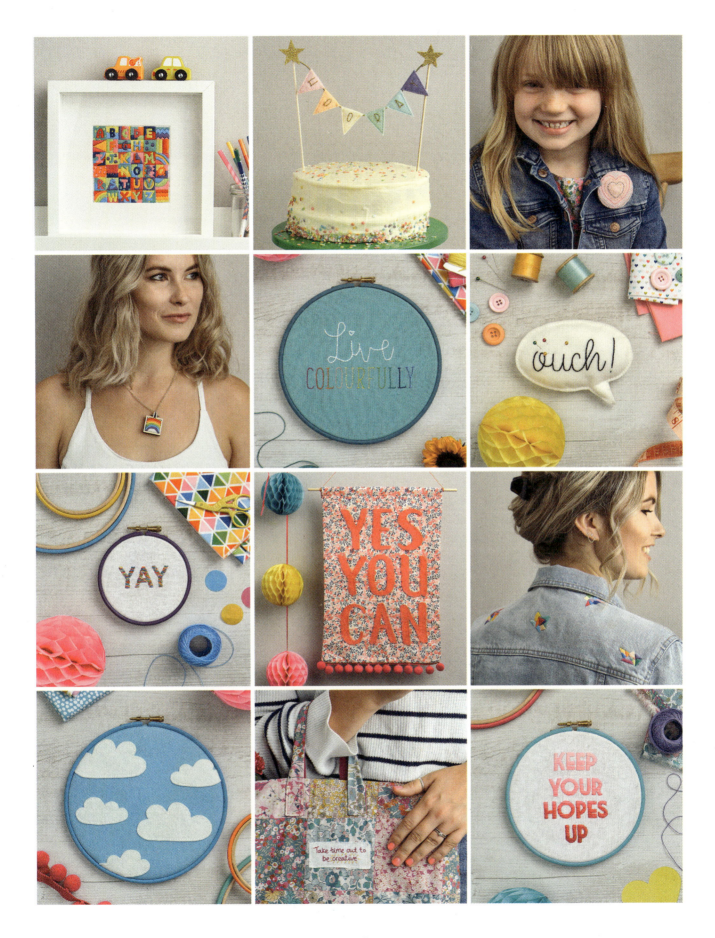

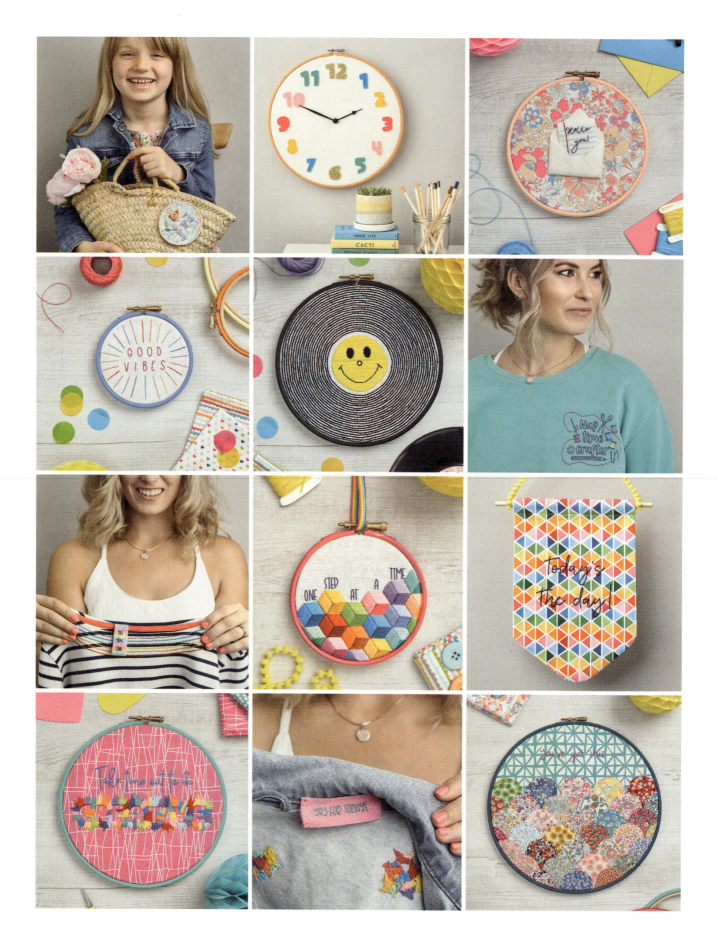

I'm open to making mistakes, then I actually find that I am more creative. Learning from your mistakes as part of the creative process is an important lesson, because that's how we learn a craft and how we develop it. I do realise it's actually really hard to embrace your mistakes, but it is something you have to get your head around to progress. Everything you create contributes in some way to the creative learning process. It is also important never to give up on being experimental – you might just discover a hidden talent or a real passion that you never knew existed within you.

During my creative journey I have also realised that you need to give yourself time to nurture your creativity. Time is something that we often feel we don't have enough of. We all have so much to do nowadays; whether it is juggling our jobs with seeing family or friends, or trying to remember exactly what it is that we need from the supermarket. It is important to recognise that any amount of time spent creating something will help you to feel good! If you don't have quite enough time to work on something one day, don't worry – instead, work out where you can find some more time the next day to continue working on it. One of the things that I absolutely love about hand embroidery is that you can pick it up and put it down as many times as you like, and it will still be there waiting for you to carry on when you can!

I have tried all sorts of crafts over the years, but really got into embroidery after my little girl was born. Once the initial brain fog had cleared after her arrival, I would sit and sew something for short amounts of time while she slept during the day, or in the evenings when she had gone to bed. The whole 'sleep while your baby sleeps' mantra never really worked for me – I felt far more energised if I had done something creative which allowed me to feel a bit more like myself again. Discovering my passion for embroidery at this time felt very energising too. I felt I had found my niche in crafting, and it made me want to do it more and more! I started to design my own patterns (something which I never would have thought I could have done before) and my confidence grew and grew. I taught myself new stitches, played around with ideas, found my own style and developed a technique that worked for me. Despite only having small amounts of time at first, that precious time helped me to discover my real passion and to really improve my overall wellbeing.

So, now let's move on to the projects in this book and start creating.

the basics

ABOUT THE PROJECTS

This book is designed to help you maximise your creative time by choosing which project you are going to work on based on how much time they take to make and how much time you have. I have divided the projects into 3 chapters: **Crafternoons**, **Medium Makes** and **Pick Me Up Projects**. Each chapter name is based on how long the featured projects might take you to finish. If you want a quick project then choose a project from the 'Crafternoons' chapter. Don't worry if you have less time, because all projects can be picked up and put down and completed at your own pace. Whether you take your time or finish them more quickly, it doesn't matter. We all work at our own pace and that's absolutely fine – don't compare yourself to anyone else. These projects are about taking the time to enjoy the creative process, and not about focusing on the end result.

Some of the 'Pick Me Up Projects' allow you to go a bit more freestyle with your work and to be more experimental, which I would encourage you to do. If you're new to hand embroidery then it might seem a bit daunting to learn a new skill in the first place, never mind being more experimental with it! Don't worry; most of the projects in this book use only a small group of basic stitches – straight stitch, backstitch, satin stitch and French knots. These stitches are extremely versatile, so once you've got the hang of them you'll be able to create so many projects and really play around and find what works for you. One of the brilliant things about hand embroidery is being able to make something completely your own and these projects have all been designed to help you do just that. Each project includes suggestions for how to make it your own by using different colours or even turning the design into a totally different project.

I hope you love stitching these projects as much as I have loved creating them for you. Remember that there is absolutely no pressure to finish them in a certain amount of time – just enjoy the creative process. It might feel like a steep learning curve at times, but exploring your creativity, finding what works for you and what you enjoy making (or what you don't!) is all part of that process. It's all about feeling good through being creative.

I wind my thread onto card bobbins, as this helps to keep them less tangled – you can buy them easily on eBay

STITCHING TIPS

Before we get started, here are a few hints and tips about hand embroidery and working on the projects in this book. You'll find lists of embroidery materials and suppliers at the back of the book, along with stitch guides to help you, but here are a few other things I think are important to understand before you begin your first project:

Embroidery thread

I always use DMC thread in my projects, so the numbers throughout the book correspond to their colour codes. The colour code numbers are the same for different types of DMC thread too, which is really handy if you want to mix the type of thread you use! If you prefer to use another brand, such as Anchor, you can find conversion charts online. I have created a DMC to Anchor conversion chart that you can download from my website, details of which are at the back of this book. Please note that projects require one skein of each colour unless otherwise stated.

Other materials

Everyone has different preferences when it comes to the type or brand of material they like to use for their embroidery projects. If you have already tried and tested something which I have not suggested, then just keep on using it! I am all for using the tools and materials that work for you. I have divided the list of embroidery materials you might need into two sections: 'essentials' and 'useful but not essential' in the Guides and Templates chapter of the book to help you choose your materials.

Test out your stitches

It's a good idea to have a scrap hoop where you can practise new stitches as many times as you like, rather than risking stitching straight on your final piece. Trust me, I've messed up SO many times, but that's how I've learnt – the hard way! Always test on the same fabric as the fabric you are using in your project, so that you can get a feel for the tension of the thread as you stitch. A 5" or 6" hoop is plenty big enough for test stitches.

Stitch selection

On each project, I suggest the stitches to use; but this isn't set in stone. Adapt the stitches you use depending on the look you want to achieve with each project. The projects in the book use a small group of stitches, but you could also add in different stitches if you are more experienced at hand embroidery.

I have a small linen fabric scrap embroidery hoop that I use to practise any new stitches

Stitching letters individually means that any stray thread in between the letters can't be seen from the front

Stitching hand lettering

When stitching a handwritten font, it's a good idea to stitch it in the same direction as you would if you were writing it. This gives a more natural feel to the text. Trace the letter with your finger before you start to make sure you're happy with the feel of it. It sounds odd, but it really makes a difference. I always have the pattern to hand so that I can check as I stitch.

It's also a good idea to stitch each letter individually, and tie off your thread at the end of each one (unless it is a joined up handwritten font). This will give a neater finish and will ensure that you can't see any stray threads through the front. This is particularly important when stitching on light coloured linen fabrics, where you can often see joins at the back from the front of the piece.

TRANSFERRING YOUR DESIGNS

There are so many ways of transferring designs onto fabric, and how you do it all comes down to personal preference. Most of the projects allow you to choose the method that works best for you, although some projects do specify a more permanent method of transfer because of the amount of time that it will take to finish the project. The following methods work well:

Tracing – if your fabric is thin enough, you can simply use a fabric pen to trace the design through the fabric. Air erasable pens work really well for this method, but you may need to keep retracing the design if you don't work quickly enough as it will start to disappear.

Tracing paper method – simply trace the design onto some lightweight tracing paper, baste or pin it onto the fabric and then stitch through the fabric. Carefully tear away the paper once the stitching is complete. This method works less well for large areas of satin stitch, but you could always stitch the outline, remove the paper and then fill it in.

Permanent transfer pens – this is my preferred way to transfer designs, as it is generally very reliable. I use Sublime Stitching fine pens and 100gsm vellum paper to transfer the designs (see my embroidery materials list in Guides and Templates at the back of the book). Just make sure that your iron is set to a cool setting with no steam, and place an old tea towel under the fabric when you iron over the vellum. You also need to reverse the design so that when you iron it on, it comes out the right way.

FINISHING THE BACK OF A HOOP

I like to leave the backs of my hoops open so that you can see all of the work that has gone into the project. I think it's really important not to worry about how the back of your work looks – you may be a neat stitcher or you may be more messy; it doesn't matter either way. Nobody sees the back anyway! Follow these steps to finish the back of your hoops my way, or use your own method if you prefer.

1. Place the finished stitching in your hoop, checking you are happy with the position of it from the front. Tighten the screw at the top with a screwdriver.

2. Using a pair of large fabric scissors, trim the excess fabric at the back to around 2.5cm (1"), or to 1.2cm

(½") for small hoops (4" or below). Follow the shape of the hoop as you cut by eye.

3. Take some perlé thread that matches your fabric colour, and measure out a length just bigger than the hoop size. Tie a knot in one end, fold over the fabric at the top of the hoop, push the needle through the fabric and make a running stitch.

4. Keep making running stitches all the way around the edge of the fabric, so the fabric starts to gather.

5. When you have gone round the whole hoop, pull the thread tight and tie in a double knot. Trim the ends to secure, and your hoop is ready to display.

chapter one: crafternoons

Who doesn't love a crafternoon – a relaxing few hours crafting and being in the moment? Grab yourself a cup of tea and a slice of your favourite cake and let yourself take time out to be creative. All the makes in this chapter can be completed in a few hours, giving you a real sense of joy in finishing a project in one sitting.

From cute mini hoops to brooches and jewellery, pincushions to bunting, these are all fun makes to make you smile. There's no pressure though; go at your own pace and enjoy the creative process.

good vibes hoop

Create your very own piece of positive hoop art with this simple but effective design. Varying the stitch length of the little star burst lines round the text brings the hoop to life. I love to think that they are spreading good vibes.

Materials:

■ 15x15cm (6x6") piece of background fabric. I like to use white linen

■ DMC embroidery thread

   3801 red

   722 orange

   17 yellow

   16 green

   959 teal

   826 blue

   209 purple

   3806 pink

   3804 pink (text colour)

■ 12.5cm (5") embroidery hoop for stitching the design in

■ 10cm (4") embroidery hoop for displaying

■ Water-based paint for the hoop (optional)

Make it your own:

■ Use a coloured or patterned fabric for the background

■ Stitch the text in a metallic thread for an extra special finish. For tips about how to sew with metallic thread, see my 'Heart Felt Brooch' project on page 21

This is one of the first patterns I designed myself when I started to focus on embroidery after Little One was born, so I really wanted to include it in my book. This 'Good Vibes Hoop' is a little positive message to hang in your home. I love that you can create individual versions of it just by mixing up the colour palette and the length of the stitches. Like several of the projects in this book, it uses just backstitch so it's perfect for a crafternoon make. There are 24 lines in the design so if you want to choose your own colours, use multiples of 2, 4, 6 or 8 different colours with a contrasting colour for the text.

INSTRUCTIONS

1. Transfer the design onto your fabric – an air erasable pen will work if you are stitching in one sitting. Use a more permanent method if not.

2. Work out which colours you are going to use where and begin by stitching the lines around the edge. Use 3 strands of thread and backstitch each line, keeping the stitch length the same along each line.

3. Repeat around the circle, varying the length of the line of stitches in each line to give it a dynamic look.

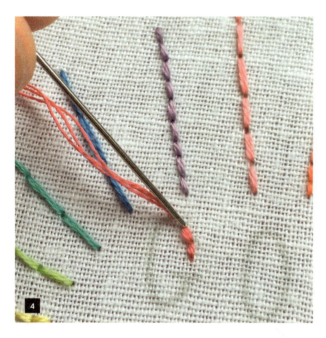

4. Stitch the text in the middle in a small backstitch using 3 strands of thread. For a really neat finish, tie a knot in the thread and trim it at the end of each letter. This stops the thread showing through the front of the hoop, especially when stitching on white linen.

5. When the stitching is complete, remove from the hoop and iron around the edge of the design (never iron over your stitching). Position in a 4" hoop to display. If you want to paint your hoop, do this before putting the finished design in the hoop.

heart felt brooch

Embroidery isn't just something that you display on your walls, you can wear it too! Create something unique with this easy to customise project. Experiment with different thread and felt colours to create a beautiful hand stitched accessory.

Materials:

- Small piece of felt – I used 'Ascot' wool felt from Cloud Craft (see suppliers list on page 134)
- DMC embroidery thread
  727 yellow
  3824 peach
  3806 pink
  747 blue
  966 mint
  E677 gold
  3689 pink (to match felt)
- Paper circle template
- A small piece of plasticard
- Brooch back
- Sharp fabric scissors

Make it your own:

- Make a heart shaped brooch with this design
- Stitch a cute character or a little doodle on your brooch
- Make a smaller version with fewer hearts or make a bigger version by stitching more hearts

I absolutely love working with felt and it's really easy to incorporate it into your embroidery projects. Felt brooches are simple but effective and quick to make, so if you want to stitch something easy that will give you the satisfying feeling of completing a project in a few hours, this is for you! The possibilities with this design are endless, so don't be afraid to adapt it yourself using different shapes or colours. Feel free not to follow the instructions exactly; give yourself permission to experiment and explore your creativity with this easy project.

I chose to use metallic thread for this brooch, as the gold makes the other colours pop. Metallic thread is notoriously difficult to stitch with, so you'll need some thread conditioner and a lot of patience! The finished effect is lovely, but don't feel you have to use it if you find it hard to work with – it's not essential.

INSTRUCTIONS

1. Trace the design onto your piece of felt. Don't worry about cutting out the shape of the brooch yet as it is much easier to stitch on a larger piece. I didn't put the felt in a hoop to stitch this design, but you can if you prefer to.

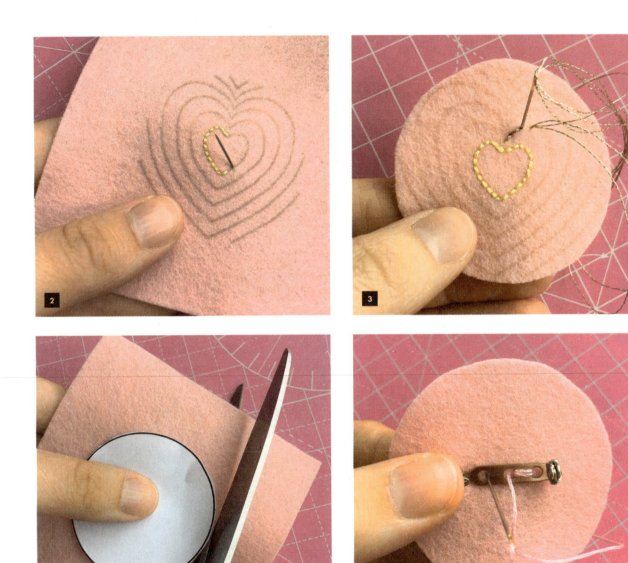

2. Select which colour you are going to use for each heart shape. Thread a needle with 3 strands of the colour you've chosen for the smallest heart in the middle and then stitch it using small backstitches.

3. Thread your needle with 3 strands of the next colour, and repeat the stitching. Continue to work outwards using the remaining colours.

4. When you've stitched all the hearts, cut out a paper circle template and place on the reverse of the felt. Position carefully so that it covers the edges of the stitching and then cut the circle out with sharp scissors. Lightly trace around the circle with with a pencil first if you prefer.

5. Cut out another circle of felt using the same

template to form the back of the brooch. Thread a needle with 3 strands of the thread that matches your felt. Attach the brooch back securely to one side of this plain felt circle.

6. Cut out a circle of plasticard, slightly smaller than the felt circles (this can be trimmed further if needed in the next step). This will make your brooch stiff.

7. Place the stitched felt right side up on top of the plain felt circle, with the brooch back on the reverse. Stitch the two together using a small backstitch and hiding the knot inside the brooch. Place the plasticard inside (trim it if required) and then backstitch around the remainder of the brooch. Tie a small knot at the back of the brooch to finish.

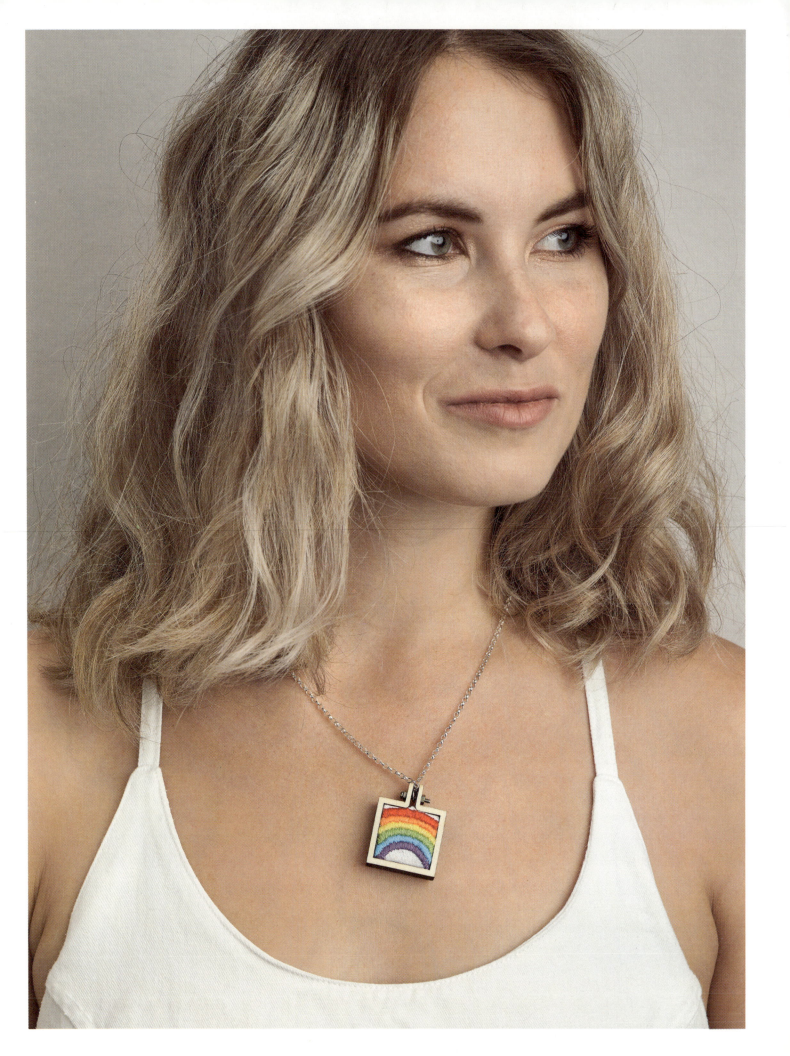

rainbow mini hoop necklace

*You don't have to be an expert at making jewellery to give this project a go –
designing this project was actually the first time that I had ever made a necklace!
You only need a few basic supplies and tools to make your own.*

Materials:

- A mini 3cm (1-1.5") embroidery hoop – I chose a square one

- A 10cm (4") embroidery hoop for stitching the design in

- White linen fabric – I used a 15x15cm (6x6") piece to fit in the 4" hoop

- DMC embroidery thread

  666 red

  970 orange

  973 yellow

  704 green

  3845 blue

  3837 purple

- A length of chain to suit your preference – I used 45cm/18"

- 6mm heavy jump rings x3

- 9mm lobster claw

- Jewellery pliers

- Super Glue

- Pencil

Make it your own:

- Choose any shape mini hoop for your necklace, or if you don't wear necklaces, make a brooch instead

I often find myself returning to a rainbow colour palette as I find it works well for so many projects. The rainbow is a symbol of hope and positivity so it's always a popular choice and the colours are just so beautiful together. Wearing a rainbow necklace is just so uplifting! I chose a square shaped hoop for this necklace, but mini hoops come in lots of different shapes so I'd recommend shopping around to find something perfect for your own jewellery project.

I always paint the hoops I use in my embroidery projects and I really wanted to paint my necklace mini hoop blue. However, after a few attempts, I found the glue used to stick the hoops together is very difficult to paint over neatly so I left it as unpainted plain wood. Putting your fabric in your mini hoop is also quite fiddly. I managed to break the first hoop, so just be really careful when it comes to assembly if this is the first time that you have used mini hoops.

INSTRUCTIONS

1. Transfer the design onto your fabric. It doesn't have to be in the centre of the fabric. You can stitch more than one design in the same hoop to save fabric.

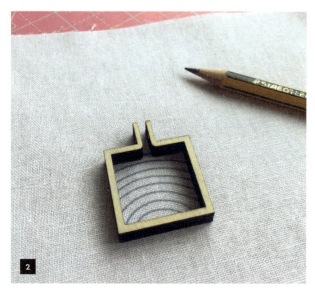

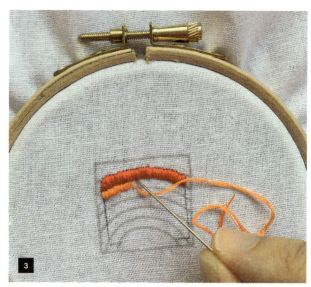

2. Take the outer frame of your mini hoop and position it over the design. Lightly draw around the inside of the frame with a pencil. Then you can place the fabric in your 10cm hoop for stitching.

3. Stitch the rainbow design with little satin stitches using 3 strands of each colour. Start with the red and work your way through the rainbow colours. Make sure that you stop stitching where you drew around the

inside of the mini hoop to avoid bulky edges.

4. When the stitching is complete, trim the fabric leaving plenty of spare fabric around the edges (leave more fabric than you think you'll need – you can't uncut it!). Place your finished rainbow stitching in the mini hoop. Check that you are happy with the positioning and adjust the hoop if needed, before trimming the edges of the fabric to 1cm.

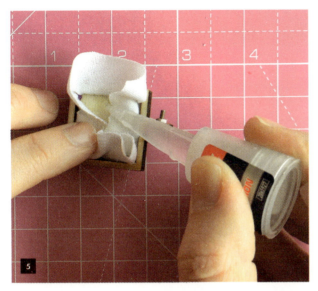

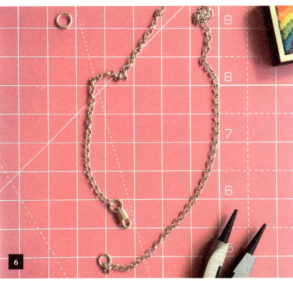

5. Very carefully, glue the excess fabric to the inside of the back of the hoop, tucking in the edges with a pencil. Keep your fingers out of the way! Glue on the back piece of the hoop to finish it. Leave it to dry completely before continuing with the next step.

6. Attach the lobster claw to a jump ring, and then fix the ring to one end of your chain. Secure with pliers. Attach another jump ring to the other end of the chain.

Work out the halfway point of the chain and attach the remaining jump ring to the middle link of the chain.

7. Put the little hoop screw through one hole at the top of the hoop, pushing it through the jump ring in the middle of the chain and then out of the hole on the other side. Secure with the nut provided (use your pliers as this can be very fiddly!).

speech bubble pincushion

Creative projects are about having fun, and this project will certainly brighten up your sewing time. It's a design that can be adapted easily and, as with all my projects, you'll find some suggestions of how to adapt it to make it your own.

Materials:
- White felt, wool or acrylic
- Black thread, shade **310**
- White thread to match your felt (there are SO many shades of white!)
- Sharp scissors
- A few pins
- A small amount of toy stuffing

Make it your own:
- Use a different colour felt and thread
- Use this design to make a felt brooch (see Heart Felt Brooch project)
- Put this design on a bag, a cushion or a jumper rather than a pincushion
- Use a phrase of your own to make a unique pincushion

Making your own sewing accessories is so easy to do, and this pincushion is a great project for a crafternoon because it's super quick. I'm always losing my pins when I work. I find if I'm sewing on the sofa, the sofa can become my pincushion, which isn't a good idea! This fun design is really versatile and there is a lot of scope to make it your own or even use the speech bubble idea to make a totally different project.

When it comes to stuffing the pincushion, I have suggested using a small amount of toy stuffing, but I tend to use stuffing from IKEA pillows. Stuffing in pillows has passed all health and safety tests, and is fine for a project like this as it is not a toy. It can be a cheaper alternative to investing in toy stuffing.

INSTRUCTIONS

1. Cut out two speech bubble shapes from the white felt. Transfer the text design onto one of the pieces.

2. To stitch the text, thread a needle with 6 strands of black thread. Stitch small backstitches along the lines of the text, starting at the top of the first letter and moving in the same direction as if you were hand writing the phrase.

3. Place the two pieces of felt together with the text facing upwards. Make sure that the pieces line up neatly. Pin them together.

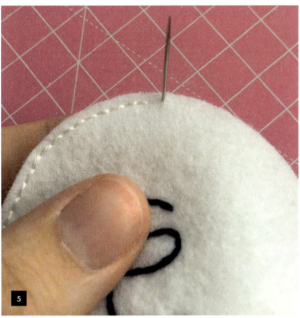

4. Thread a needle with 3 strands of white thread. Stitch the two pieces of felt together with backstitch a few millimetres away from the edge. Leave a 4cm (2") gap to allow you to stuff the pincushion.

5. Stuff the pincushion, starting with small amounts in the point of the bubble before filling in the rest. Close the opening by continuing the backstitch in white thread along the open edge.

happy clothes labels

You don't need dressmaking experience to add a special finishing touch to a garment. These happy clothes labels are such an easy way to add personality. Sew one into your child's jumper to give them a little positive boost every day.

Materials:

- A 12cm (5") piece of cotton ribbon or webbing (15mm or 25mm width works well)
- 7.5cm (3") embroidery hoop for stitching. Use a longer bit of ribbon if you have a 10cm (4") hoop
- Contrasting embroidery thread
- A couple of pins
- An iron
- Sharp fabric scissors

Make it your own:

- Experiment with different ribbons
- Make a vertical label
- Use your own choice of phrase
- Experiment with stitching little pictures onto your labels too

Sometimes it's nice to find a little bit of motivation in an unexpected place. Writing a little note to yourself can give you a real boost, especially if you've got a difficult day ahead. I think what motivates us is a very personal thing; some people need public affirmation to help motivate them, whilst some people have more private sources of motivation. I think this is a lovely project whichever category you fit into.

These labels are really easy to make and are a great stash buster too – the ribbon in the 'you look lovely today' design comes from a Mollie Makes magazine cover project many years ago. Choose cotton ribbon or webbing, as shiny satin ribbons are difficult to stitch on. Add to your design by stitching a little picture to complement your motivational phrase. Whatever you choose, you'll see a little bit of happiness every time you put on your clothes!

INSTRUCTIONS

1. Transfer the design onto the middle of a piece of cotton ribbon or webbing, and place it in your hoop. This does feel a bit odd at first as it can be tricky to

get it in position, but stick with it – you'll just need to maintain tension as you stitch.

2. Thread a needle with 2 strands of your chosen thread colour (I used 3340 here). Stitch in very small backstitch over the lines of each letter. Usually I would suggest tying your thread off at the end of each letter, but it doesn't matter for this project. Just make sure you trim off any loose thread at the back of the ribbon.

3. When complete, remove the ribbon from the hoop and press the ends of the ribbon (but not the stitching)

with a cool iron. Trim the ends so that you have around 1cm spare at either side. Fold 0.5cm over at each end and press again.

4. Take your garment (mine is the Naptime Crafter Sweatshirt – see page 78) and position the label. You could remove the original label as I have here, or leave it in if you prefer. Pin the middle in position, leaving either end free for stitching. Stitch each end in position with 3 strands of matching colour thread (I have used 958 here) using a small backstitch. Remove the pin and it's ready to wear!

I love giving my clothes a personal touch. Here I've sewn my 'Yay for Today' clothes label onto my customised denim jacket project on page 108

live colourfully hoop

Larger hoops don't have to be complicated to look beautiful. This hoop combines simple text and a plain background to make the little details stand out. Tie some ribbon through the top to display, or add some pom poms for an extra flourish.

Materials:
- 27x27cm (roughly 11x11") teal linen fabric
- DMC embroidery thread:
  917 magenta
  3801 red
  970 orange
  3824 peach
  744 pale yellow
  973 yellow
  165 pale green
  703 bright green
  3812 bright teal
  796 dark blue
  3838 cornflower blue
  white (blanc)
- 18cm (7") embroidery hoop
- Water-based paint for the hoop (optional)
- Teal perlé thread to match the fabric. I used shade **3814**

Make it your own:
- Stitch the design as a banner, or on a jumper or sweatshirt
- Experiment with your own colour palette
- Stitch the design in one colour on patterned fabric

One of the main features of my style and my work is colour! I absolutely love playing around with different colour palettes and combinations of hues. In fact, I very rarely stitch in black. This simple hoop is a lovely way to celebrate colour in everyday life. I decided to use the same teal colour for the fabric and the painted hoop to make the lettering really stand out, but you can make this design as muted or colourful as you like!

To create a little bit of contrast, I used 6 strands of white thread for the word 'live' to make it thicker. It can sometimes be a bit tricky to thread a needle with 6 strands (I get asked about how to do this all the time when I'm teaching my workshops!). You might need a longer needle with a bigger eye to fit the 6 strands through, or you could try a needle threader. If all else fails, just wet the end of your thread to make it easier to get through the eye.

INSTRUCTIONS

1. Transfer the design onto your fabric and place it securely in the hoop. Thread a needle with 6 strands of white thread.

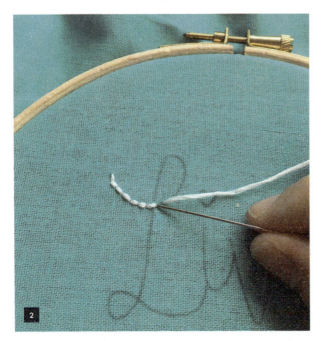

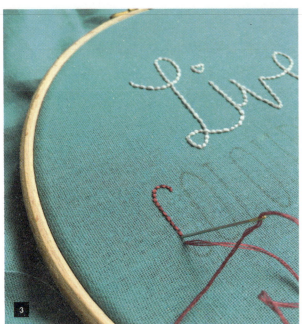

2. Stitch over the letters in small backstitch, following the direction of the writing as if you were writing it by hand. Using white stitching on a coloured background means your stitches will really stand out, so try to keep them nice and evenly sized if you can.

3. The word 'colourfully' is stitched using 3 strands of thread, starting with magenta (917) for the letter

'C'. Stitch using very small backstitches along the line of the letters, keeping the size of your stitches as consistent as possible. Repeat in a different colour thread for all the remaining letters in the word.

4. Finish the back of your hoop (see my preferred method of finishing the back of your hoop on page 13). I have used a matching perlé thread to sew the back of this hoop to give a neat finish.

yay mini hoop

A mini 10cm (4") hoop is the perfect-sized project to take out and about and enjoy stitching on the go. This project is particularly easy to transport and stitch as it is constructed quite freely around the basic outline of the lettering.

Materials:

- A 15x15cm (6x6") piece of white linen fabric
- 10cm (4") embroidery hoop
- A selection of loose ends of threads from your stash
- Water-based paint for the hoop (optional)

Make it your own:

- Use a plain colour or patterned fabric for the background
- Stitch the design with a few shades of the same colour or a select colour palette to build up the lettering
- Choose specific colours! This doesn't have to be stitched with loose ends of threads if you prefer to choose your palette

This is the first of my 'loose ends' projects – a project which helps you to use up all of those spare bits of thread left over from other projects. Until fairly recently I didn't keep any of my loose ends and just threw them away. It always felt like a bit of a waste, especially if I had quite a lot left on a strand I had finished with, so I decided to keep them in a jar until they were needed for something! I love seeing the colours build up from other projects, and it's great to have a rummage in the jar for a colour when you eventually use them. One thing about using loose ends is that you don't know exactly which colour numbers you are using, so you're guaranteed to have something unique when you stitch a project with them.

This 'mini' hoop is actually a 10cm (4") hoop, but you could use a bigger hoop if you prefer. The lettering is built up by layering different threads, so you could make this in an afternoon or take more time over it if you prefer. The finished effect makes the text really stand out from the fabric.

INSTRUCTIONS

1. Transfer the design onto your fabric and place it securely in your embroidery hoop. Choose your first colour from your loose ends and thread a needle.

41

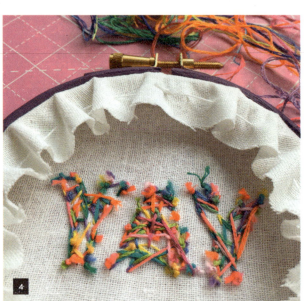

2. Bring the needle up through the fabric along the outer edge of the first letter 'Y'. Make a straight stitch in any direction, and repeat a few times in different places and directions on the same letter. Tie a knot at the back and trim. Repeat on the remaining letters (I like to put a small amount of each colour on each of the letters so that there is some continuity, but you don't have to do this at all).

3. Repeat with more colours, layering up the thread in different directions and filling in the gaps.

4. When you are happy with the coverage, you are ready to finish the back of your hoop.

bunting cake topper

No celebration would be complete without some bunting! There is something lovely about miniature bunting and it looks so good on top of a cake. If you don't want to stitch the text then just leave it out – the bunting will still look great.

Materials:

- Felt: ascot, apricot, buttery, pistachio, spearmint, lavender posie and gold glitter (wool felt from Cloud Craft – see suppliers on page 134)

- DMC embroidery thread:
  3689 pink
  3856 orange
  3078 yellow
  966 mint
  3811 blue
  155 purple
  E3852 gold

- A few pins

- 2 bamboo kebab skewers

- Blu tack

- A rug needle (or a similar long and blunt needle)

- 55cm gold cord ribbon

- A pencil

- Super Glue

Make it your own:

- Personalise it with a name or different phrase

- Put mini pom poms on the tops of the skewers

- Change the shape of the bunting flags

I really love baking cakes and wanted to find a fun way to incorporate my love of cooking into one of my projects without embroidering a cupcake! Cake toppers have been around for a while, but I thought it would be great to have an embroidered topper that could be used for lots of special occasions. It's lovely to make something that can be used time and time again. This design would work for so many celebrations and can be personalised easily too.

The bunting is permanently attached to the skewers, so just be careful when washing them after taking them out of the cake (the felt bunting won't take kindly to being placed in a bowl of water). Wash the skewers before you make the project, and then wipe with a cloth after placing in your cake.

INSTRUCTIONS

1. Cut out the felt bunting shapes and transfer the letter design onto each one, remembering to make 2 of the letter 'O'. The letter should be positioned a little way down each flag. You might find it helpful to line up all of the flags to check that the letters are positioned evenly.

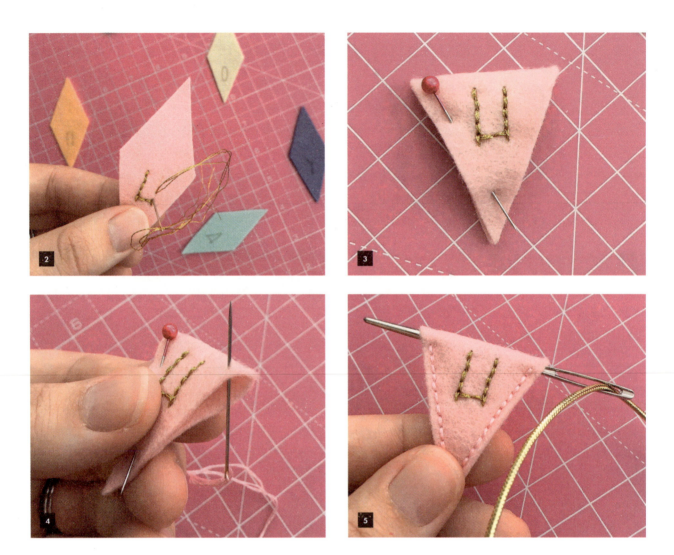

2. Thread a needle with 3 strands of the gold thread. This can be quite tricky, so keep your strands of thread fairly short (no longer than around 25cm/10") and use thread conditioner to keep the strands together. Stitch each letter using a small backstitch.

3. Take the first letter flag and fold it in half so the letter is on the outside and the triangles are lined up neatly. Pin it together and then thread a needle with 3 strands of thread to match the fabric (this is 3689 to match the pink felt) trimming the end close to the knot.

4. Sew the triangles together, starting the stitching a few millimetres from the top of the folded edge so that the cord can be threaded through the top of each flag. Make a small stitch through both layers of felt, and then stitch using backstitch all the way around the flag. Remember to leave a gap at the top for the cord.

5. Make sure you match the thread to the felt colour as you stitch your flags together. When you have made all your flags, thread them onto the cord using a rug needle (or use a similar blunt needle with a big enough eye to thread the cord through).

6. Cut your skewers to size if they are too long. You then need to glue the cord to the skewers. Because you are using Super Glue, it's important to keep the bunting and your fingers out of the way. I find it is best to work on a covered, flat surface whilst working with Super Glue. Work out the width of the cord and then wrap it tightly about 2cm around the top of the skewers to measure where you will be gluing your cord.

7. Put some Super Glue on the skewer and then carefully wrap the cord tightly around it, trimming off

any excess cord. Press down on the cord for a minute or two just to check it has stuck. Repeat with the other skewer. When you have glued both ends use blobs of blu tack on the bottom of each skewer and stand them up on a flat surface to leave them to dry.

8. When dry, cut out two star shapes from the gold glitter felt and stick them on the top of the skewers to cover up the cord. Once this is also dry, rearrange your bunting so it is evenly distributed. Pop it in a cake and let the celebrations begin!

chapter two: medium makes

This next chapter features projects that you can take a little more time over. They might take you a few days to complete, but there's absolutely no pressure to finish any of my makes in a certain amount of time! If you prepare at home first, some of these projects are great to take out and about with you. I used to regularly take sewing to do on my lunch break. I find snatching even a few minutes of sewing time really helps my wellbeing. I have also been told that watching me stitch helps other people relax too; maybe embroidery should be a new spectator sport?

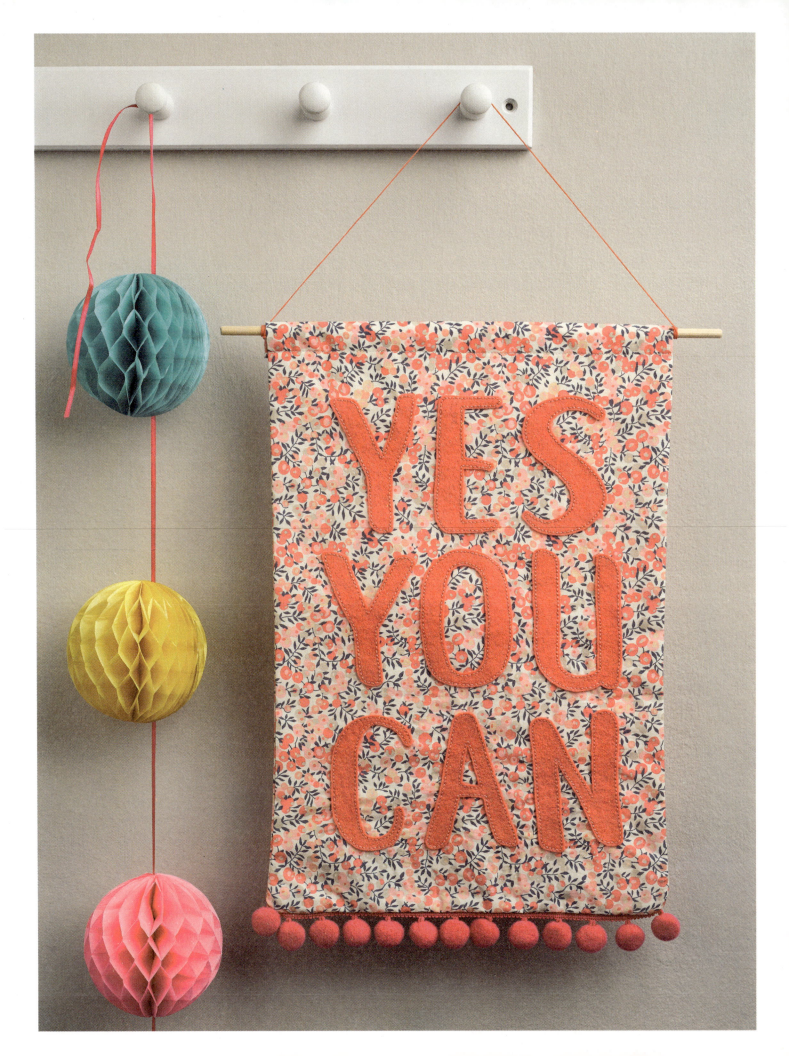

yes you can banner

This is a project that you have to stay at home to enjoy making. It is perfect for rainy days when you need to stay in. I used my sewing machine to put the banner together, but you could stitch it by hand if you prefer.

Materials:
- Two pieces of patterned fabric, measuring 34x47cm
- Two pieces of lightweight interfacing, measuring 30x42cm
- Felt for the lettering
- Sharp fabric scissors
- An iron
- Fabric adhesive, such as a spray or Wondaweb
- Thread to match the felt – I used 2 skeins of **893**
- 35cm decorative trim
- Sewing machine
- Cotton thread to match the fabric – I used cream
- Dowel, at least 40cm in length
- String to hang your banner

Make it your own:
- Use contrasting thread to stitch the letters
- Use different colours of felt for the lettering
- Stitch a different motivational phrase

I used to think that motivational quotes could be a bit twee, but over the last few years I've actually found that some of them really work for me. A positive message or affirmation can really help if you're going through a difficult time or have a difficult day ahead of you (on other days they don't work at all, and that's fine too!). If there's a phrase that you find helps you then it's good to be reminded of it regularly, which is why I created this large banner.

This banner is just slightly smaller than A3, but you could make it smaller if you prefer (there is a template for a smaller one in my 'Double-sided Banner' project on page 62). By attaching the felt letters to the banner before stitching, you can make this as a medium make or take more time over it if you wish.

INSTRUCTIONS

1. Iron both pieces of patterned fabric to remove any creases. Attach the pieces of interfacing onto the reverse (following manufacturer's instructions), leaving roughly 5 cm (2") around the top edge and 2.5cm (1") around the sides.

51

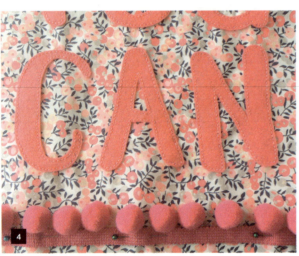

2. Carefully cut out the letters from the felt using sharp fabric scissors, and then position them on the right side of one of the pieces of patterned fabric. Remember that the top will be turned over, so don't place the letters too close to the top. Use fabric adhesive to attach the letters to the fabric.

3. Thread a needle with 3 strands of thread, and then stitch using small backstitches around the edges of each letter. Keep the stitches around 2-3mm from the edge of the felt.

4. When the letters are secure, you can assemble the banner. Take a piece of decorative trim and position it on the bottom of the front piece of the banner, with the trim pointing upwards (i.e. pom poms at the top). Stitch along the tape and then trim off any pom poms or trim that falls outside the outer seam.

5. Place the back of the banner on top of the front, right sides together. Pin together a couple of centimetres from the edge, making sure that you aren't trapping the letters or the trim inside the seams. The pom poms or trim should be pointing upwards inside.

6. Carefully stitch down the sides and along the bottom edge of the banner, leaving the top open. Take your time along the bottom edge as it can be quite bulky, especially if you have used pom pom trim.

7. Turn it right side out to check you are happy with seam placement. Then turn it inside out again, trim the seams to 1cm and clip the corners diagonally so the banner lies flat when turned right side out.

8. Iron the banner with a very cool iron with no steam, being careful to avoid the lettering and the pom poms.

9. Trim any loose thread away from the top edge and then turn over 4cm of fabric and press. Turn 1cm of this underneath and press again – this will create the opening for the dowel. Pin in place and check that your dowel fits through, before stitching along the bottom edge of the turned over fabric.

10. Adjust the length of the dowel if necessary, and sand the ends so that they are smooth. Place it through the opening you have made, and tie a length of string to each end to hang.

blue skies hoop

Felt is a great material for bigger craft projects as well as smaller ones. I love the textures you can create by layering felt – don't be afraid to add more design elements to this project if you're feeling creative.

Materials:

- 20x20cm (8x8") pieces of blue and white felt
- White thread (either blanc or another shade – **3865** matches my felt)
- A few pins
- Sharp fabric scissors
- A 7" embroidery hoop
- Blue water-based paint for the hoop (optional)
- A pencil

Make it your own:

- Draw your own cloud shapes for something completely unique
- Add a sun, rainbow or another weather element

I first had the idea for this hoop on a really gloomy January day. It was one of those days surrounded by lots of other gloomy days when all I needed was to see a bit of sun and blue sky! I decided to take matters into my own hands and make my own blue skies. I don't like wishing away the seasons (although it's hard not to in January), so this is the perfect way to have a little blue sky every day.

I use my hoop as a pin hoop to display all of my rainbow themed pins. Pins are like little works of art, so I love to have them on display. Once you have a collection, you won't be able to stop!

INSTRUCTIONS

1. Pin the cloud templates onto the white felt. Carefully cut out 2 big cloud shapes and 3 smaller ones, trimming away any slightly square edges once the template has been removed.

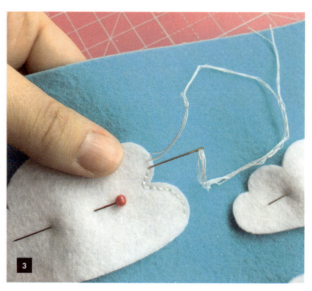

2. Place the embroidery hoop on top of the blue felt. Position the clouds so they are spread evenly around the hoop (some may be half in and half out, which is fine!). Once you're happy, pin the clouds in place.

3. Stitch the clouds to the felt using 3 strands of embroidery thread, using small backstitches all the way round each cloud, around 2mm from the edge. Repeat until all of the clouds are attached.

4. Paint your hoop at this point if you wish. I painted this hoop in two coats of a blue that complements the felt colour, or use a contrasting colour if you prefer.

5. Once your hoop is dry, position the square of felt inside and then tighten. Use a pencil to draw around the edge on the reverse of the hoop. Take the felt out, trim around the felt and then reposition back in the hoop before tightening it.

snail mail hoop

This is a great stash-busting project – if you're anything like me then you'll have plenty of fabric that you bought because you loved the print but weren't sure what to make with it. Any fabric with a small print will work well with this hoop.

Materials:
- White felt, measuring roughly 21 x 14cm (8x6")
- 22x22cm (9x9") patterned fabric for the background
- 15cm (6") embroidery hoop
- DMC embroidery thread:
  162 light blue
  321 red
  824 dark blue
  plus white to match felt
- Sharp fabric scissors
- Water-based paint for the hoop (optional)

Make it your own:
- Use your own text for a special occasion
- Make a snail mail envelope brooch (see 'Heart Felt Brooch' on page 20)
- Stitch a double-sided letter with a secret message on the back. Remember not to secure the letter in position in step 7 if you are going to do this

I really love sending a letter (snail mail), and it's something that I should do more often. It's so nice to spend time handwriting letters on pretty stationery and posting them in a handmade envelope (check out my blog for my envelope making tutorial). This little hoop is a way of sending an extra special piece of snail mail which can also be displayed in your home. It's another project that can be personalised in so many ways, and can be sent as a gift for a special occasion.

The stitching on the letter combines the use of 2 and 3 strands to achieve the finer details. If you have never used just 2 strands before, have a little practice on some spare felt before you stitch the real thing.

INSTRUCTIONS

1. Place the piece of patterned background fabric into your hoop and tighten. Cut out the envelope shape from your felt and then position and pin it onto the fabric. You might find it helpful to fold up the sides and the bottom of the envelope to check you have the correct position.

59

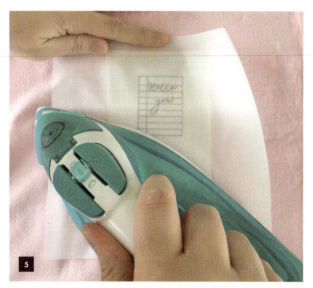

2. Thread your needle with 3 strands of white thread, and stitch the rectangle that forms the back of the envelope onto the fabric with a small backstitch.

3. Fold in one side of the envelope and then fold the bottom edge on top of that. With the same thread, bring your needle up through the bottom of the envelope (inside so the end is hidden), and then stitch it together with more little backstitches. You can pin

this together if you like, but I found it to be more of a hassle! Repeat on the other side of the envelope, but leave the top section unstitched.

4. Secure the sides of the envelope by putting a small stitch in the top corners.

5. To make the letter, transfer the design onto the felt and cut it out, leaving plenty of space around the

edge. You can leave enough to fit it into a small hoop if you prefer.

6. The letter is also stitched using backstitch – keep your stitches nice and small on this project. The paper lines are stitched with 3 strands of blue and red thread. Stitch the blue horizontal lines first and the vertical red one on top. The text should be stitched last, using 2 strands of dark blue thread.

7. Once stitched, trim the edges of the felt to be level with the ends of your stitches. Be very careful when doing this and make sure that your scissors are nice and sharp. Check that the letter fits in the envelope.

8. Secure the letter in the hoop with a couple of small stitches at the bottom so they are hidden inside the envelope. Finish the back of the hoop and it is ready to display.

double-sided banner

This is a smaller banner project than the Yes You Can Banner. When I had the idea of stitching on the reverse, I wondered why I hadn't considered it before. When I have my own studio space, I will make an open/closed version for the door.

Materials:
- Two pieces of patterned fabric, measuring 33x23cm (13x9")
- Two pieces of lightweight interfacing, banner template-shaped
- 1 skein of thread for the text – I used **823**
- An iron
- Sewing machine and thread to match your fabric
- A length of dowel
- A hacksaw
- Twine or trim to hang
- A small piece of sandpaper

Make it your own:
- Make a straight edge along the bottom and add pom pom trim
- Make a small single-sided banner instead
- Use this design to make a hoop

Sometimes it's easy to feel like you should always be having a good day. When you are looking at someone else's Instagram feed or other social media channel it's easy to fall into the comparison trap and feel everyone else is living a better life than you. It is absolutely okay not to be okay – nobody has a great day every day. I designed this project for both good and bad days; and you can just flip it over depending on your mood!

I really wanted to use pom pom trim on this project as I had the most perfect mini trim in my stash. It was actually really hard to stitch it along the bottom edge of this banner with the curved, pointed edge (never mind writing the instructions!), so I have used my pom pom trim to hang the banner instead. You can always use some twine or cord if you prefer.

INSTRUCTIONS

1. Transfer the designs onto the right side of your fabric, one onto each piece. Make sure that they are centred and that you are happy with the positioning by using the paper template as a guide.

2. Following the manufacturer's instructions, iron the interfacing onto the back of the fabric. Leave a gap of around 4-5cm at the top. Backstitch over the lettering using 3 strands of thread. As with the other hand lettering projects in this book, follow the lines of the letters as though you were writing by hand. Repeat on the other side of the banner. You can stitch the lettering with the fabric in a hoop and then iron it afterwards, being careful to avoid the lettering.

3. Trim the fabric to 0.5cm around the side edges of

the interfacing on both pieces of your banner. Do not trim the top as you will need this to feed the dowel through to hang your banner.

4. Place the right sides of both pieces together and then pin them in position, leaving the top open.

5. Stitch along the side edges on your sewing machine, 0.5cm inside the edge of the interfacing, using a straight stitch.

6. Trim the remaining fabric around the side edges, following the line of the interfacing. Leave the top for now. Clip the curved corners by cutting a few small triangles from the seam allowance, being careful not to cut too close to the stitching.

7. Turn the right way out and press, avoiding ironing the lettering on both sides. Trim any loose threads from the top edge and turn over 3.5cm, pressing again.

8. Turn 1cm underneath and press to create the

opening for the dowel, checking first it fits. Pin in place and stitch close to the bottom edge using your sewing machine.

9. Place the dowel through the opening and cut a length you are happy with using a hacksaw. Sand the ends so that they are smooth. Finally, tie twine to each side of the dowel to hang your banner. I secured the pom pom trim to my banner using a couple of small stitches. Check that the dowel still fits through. Your banner is finished!

rainbow yoke

This is the first of two projects in this chapter to customise your clothing. Hand embroidery is an easy way to add unique details to your clothes. Everyone's version of this will be different because of the style of garment and free design.

Materials:

- A garment to stitch – a cotton top, t-shirt or sweatshirt would work well

- Some lightweight interfacing for around the neckline

- An iron

- DMC embroidery thread:

  817 red

  721 orange

  18 yellow

  911 green

  3844 blue

  552 purple

- An air erasable pen (optional)

Make it your own:

- Use satin stitch to create bolder stripes

- Stitch around the cuffs or bottom edge of your garment

- Stitch a geometric design around the neckline – have a look at my 'Customised Denim Jacket' on page 108 for inspiration

You've probably guessed by now that rainbows feature quite a lot in my work! I also love a good Breton stripe top (I probably have way too many of them), and wanted to combine the two to show how easy it is to jazz up your wardrobe with embroidery. You'll firstly need to wash the garment that you are going to customise before you start stitching and again afterwards.

There aren't any templates for this project as it is best to go freestyle. That might sound a bit daunting if you're used to working with a pattern, but don't worry! Because what you choose will have a different neckline than the example here, you need to work out the project based on your garment. You can play around with colours too. I decided to stitch purple closest to my face so that I can see the rainbow when I look down, but you can do it whichever way round you prefer.

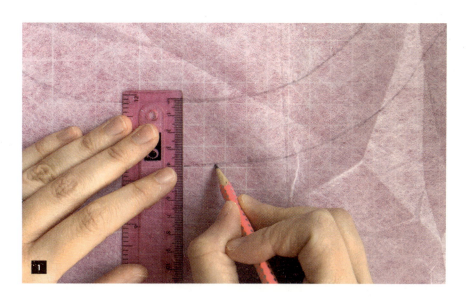

INSTRUCTIONS

1. Turn your garment inside out. Mark the line of the neckline on the interfacing with a pencil. Cut the interfacing following the line so it is around 4cm deep and just covers the shoulder seam. Iron on the inside of the front neckline following manufacturer's instructions, ensuring it is not visible.

2. Each of the rainbow lines are stitched with backstitch using 6 strands of thread. I started with the purple first, a little way down from the top of the neckline, following the overlocking stitches on the hem of the neckline. Make sure that the thread goes through the shoulder seams at either end, as this gives a lovely neat finish when all the colours have been stitched.

3. Repeat with the remaining colours of the rainbow. I covered the bottom line of the stitching on the hem

of the neckline with blue, and then worked out the spacing for the rest of the colours by eye, based on the distance between the purple and blue rows (roughly 6mm apart). It's important to ensure that all the stitching is done on the area you have interfaced. If you prefer, you can draw the lines with an air erasable pen just to make sure.

4. Take care when washing your garment once it has been stitched. Wash at a low temperature, using a colour catcher to make sure the colours don't run.

Once complete, you could add a 'Happy Clothes Label' to add a little extra personalised touch inside! See page 33 for details

keep your hopes up hoop

Satin stitch lends itself so well to blending colours together; the impact is really effective. Have a look at my guide to satin stitch at the back of this book, as getting your stitches perfect will help you to achieve a smoother overall finish.

Materials:

- 22x22cm (roughly 9x9") white linen fabric

- DMC embroidery thread in pinks:

  605

  604

  603

  602

  601

  600

- A 15cm (6") embroidery hoop

- A permanent method of design transfer

- Water-based paint for the hoop (optional)

- An iron

Make it your own:

- Choose your own colour palette – there are some ideas on my blog if you want a place to start

- Stitch an ombré design on a banner or a bag

- Experiment with patterned fabrics for an even more colourful hoop

I saw the phrase "keep your hopes up" on Pinterest a little while ago, and it really resonated with me. More often we hear people saying "don't get your hopes up", and it made me wonder why. Why not keep your hopes up? With all the uncertainty in the world at the moment, it's good to look for positives where we can!

Ombré stitching is one of my favourite lettering styles to stitch, and it is perfect for this project. When choosing a colour palette, don't try to use too many different colours; it is much better to have a good blend of shades so the graduation and blend of colours shine through. I've stuck to a pink palette here, but experiment with your own too. You'll need to keep your thread organised as you stitch this, so keep any loose bits on a card bobbin.

INSTRUCTIONS

1. Transfer the design onto your fabric and then place in the embroidery hoop. Keep the fabric tight in the hoop throughout stitching, but not so tight that it stretches out of shape.

71

2. Before you start stitching, work out your colour placement. I used light to dark colours from top to bottom on this project, but you could do it the other way around if you prefer.

3. Thread a needle with 3 strands of the colour you want to use for the top of the word 'keep' (I used 605). Stitch a block of satin stitch from the top of the letter to a little way down (1cm or so), stitching just outside the lines of the letters. Repeat for the whole word 'keep'.

4. Take the second colour (604) and repeat step 3 at the bottom of the letters, leaving a gap between the two colour blocks.

5. Repeat step 4 until all colours have been used, leaving a gap between the colour blocks.

6. Next blend the colours together. Working from the top, take the first shade and make a few stitches away from the first block colour towards the second. Your stitches should have gaps in between that increase in size – you could also make one or two stitches a little way into the second block of colour.

7. Repeat with the remaining colours until they are blended together. Add a little of the colour from the bottom of the word 'your' to the top of the word 'hopes' and vice versa, to blend the colours between the top and bottom half.

8. Remove the fabric from the hoop and press the edges with an iron. Paint your hoop at this point if you wish. I used a vibrant turquoise, as it's my favourite colour with pink. Place the fabric back in the hoop, then position and tighten before finishing the back.

73

easy peasy patches

This is another project where you can raid your fabric stash to find just what you need. It is worth using the two different sizes of hoop if you can – the smaller one will give you better tension for stitching the edging around the patch.

Materials:
- 18x18cm (7x7") piece of patterned cotton fabric
- 8x18cm (3x7") piece of lightweight interfacing
- 18x18cm (7x7") piece of felt (in any colour you like)
- An iron
- Loose ends of thread
- One 10cm (4") and one 12.5cm (5") embroidery hoop
- Sharp scissors

Make it your own:
- The design possibilities for patches are endless really, so have a go at designing your own
- You could document the places you have visited by making a patch for each destination and sewing them onto a travel bag
- Stitch a patch for special occasions

Patches have really become popular again recently, and it's actually very easy to make your own. They are a really great way of expressing yourself, and are very versatile craft projects. If you haven't got a pin collection then you might want to start your own patch collection! I love to sew them on jeans, denim jackets and, as you can see here, bags. Kids love badges so they are a great present to make for any little ones in your life.

I've suggested you use your loose ends of threads for this project, but you can always pick out specific colours if you prefer. The only colour I specifically chose for this project was the colour for the satin stitching around the edge, because I wanted it to complement the fabric.

INSTRUCTIONS
1. Iron the background fabric to remove any creases, and then secure the interfacing on the back (following manufacturer's instructions). Transfer the design, including the outer circle, onto the patterned fabric and place in a 5" embroidery hoop.

2. As this is a loose ends project, I have used slightly different shades for the flower petals and the leaves, but it is all stitched using 3 strands of thread. Here are some tips on how to stitch each part of the design:

■ Stitch the flower face first, using backstitch for the mouth and French knots for the eyes.

■ Use backstitch to stitch the circle of the flower. Stitch around the edge of the circle working inwards until

completely covered, working carefully around the face. This gives a lovely texture to the centre of the flower.

■ The petals are stitched using satin stitch, working from the tips of the petals towards the centre of the flower.

■ The text is stitched last, using small backstitches. I used shade 3838 for these – it's one of my favourite shades and I had a lot of it in my loose ends jar!

3. When you have finished your stitching, remove it from the 5" hoop. Take the inner ring of the 4" hoop, place the felt and the stitched fabric on top and secure the outer ring.

4. Now you can stitch the two pieces together with an edging satin stitch around the drawn outer circle. Thread a needle with your chosen thread (I picked shade 20 instead of using loose ends), and bring it up through the back of the fabric, 2-3mm from the outside

edge. Push the needle back down just inside the edge of the circle to cover the pencil line. Stitch all the way round in satin stitch, ensuring you fill the gaps for a neat finish (see stitch guide on page 117).

5. Remove from the hoop. Carefully trim the edges with your sharp scissors, as close as you possible to the edge.

6. Your patch is ready to stitch onto a jacket or bag!

naptime crafter sweatshirt

Stitching on stretch fabrics is notoriously tricky, but the Magic Paper that I used on this sweatshirt is fantastic and really stabilises the fabric. Use a fine permanent marker pen to trace the design as it won't run when you wash the fabric.

Materials:
- A sweatshirt, washed and ironed
- DMC Magic Paper (see suppliers list for more information)
- DMC embroidery thread:
  336 dark blue
  917 magenta
  3746 purple
  16 green
  995 bright blue
- A 16x16cm (roughly 6x6") piece of lightweight interfacing
- A 20cm (8") embroidery hoop for stitching in
- A bowl of water

Make it your own:
- Stitch the design onto a different garment or a fabric bag
- Make a banner or brooch
- You could use satin stitch to fill in some of the design

Since Little One was born, I have become a naptime crafter. When she was really small, I used to pop her in the sling for a nap and do a bit of stitching or blogging. As she started sleeping in her cot during the day, I was able to do a bit more stitching. Having a little bit of creative time in the day really helped me in so many ways; mainly because it helped me to feel like me.

I created this design to celebrate all the naptime crafters out there. Keep snatching those golden minutes to be creative, whether it's 10 minutes, 30 minutes or even longer if you have a good sleeper! Be creative with how you stitch this design; you could include more colour than I have here. You could even include a 'Happy Clothes Label' too.

INSTRUCTIONS

1. Trace the pattern (right way around) onto a blank piece of Magic Paper, using a fine permanent marker. When you've done this, position on the sweatshirt before peeling off the backing and sticking in place on the front.

79

2. Iron the piece of interfacing onto the reverse of the sweatshirt, making sure that the design on the front is completely covered. Don't use any steam to do this. The Magic Paper instructions don't require you to use interfacing, but I think it's helpful for stitching on this stretchy fabric.

3. Thread a needle with 3 strands of the dark blue thread, and stitch around the edges of the text using small backstitches.

4. The remaining elements of the design are stitched in the same colour as the text, but with 2 strands of thread instead of 3 (except for the eye of the needle, where I used 1 strand of thread). Stitch the frame

around the design in a different colour for contrast. I used 917 (my absolute favourite colour!).

5. When you have covered all of the design, you can do the magic with the Magic Paper! Place the sweatshirt in a bowl of lukewarm water and watch it disappear. When the paper has all dissolved , carefully squeeze out any excess water and leave the sweatshirt to dry.

6. Once dry, stitch a few strands of thread on each of the bobbins, using 3 strands of thread. Make sure you stitch the bobbin on the left in the same colour as the thread that goes around the edge of the design and you're done!

I washed my sweatshirt on a 15 minute cycle after the stitching was complete, just to make the stitched area soft again. Remember not to iron over the design at any point

chapter three: pick me up projects

The final chapter of this book is all about really taking your time over your crafting. Sometimes we are so keen to finish a project we forget to enjoy the creative process. For me, the pleasure in the making is as important as the delight in the end result.

From mixing patchwork with embroidery to making a customised denim jacket and artworks to hang in your home, I hope you enjoy working on these 'Pick Me Up Projects' and that they help you to feel more energised, motivated and, most importantly, happy.

long player hoop

This project is great if you need something to work on that doesn't require a lot of concentration, as most of it involves stitching round and round the circles of the LP. Simple but very effective, this design is something to be treasured and enjoyed.

Materials:
- 27x27cm (10x10") piece of white linen
- Permanent method of design transfer
- 5 skeins of black thread, shade **310**
- 1 skein of yellow thread, shade **307**
- A 20cm (8") and a 18cm (7") embroidery hoop
- Black water-based paint for the hoop (optional but recommended)

Make it your own:
- Make a smiley patch (see page 74) or a felt brooch (page 20) for the middle of your LP
- Stitch a label with your favourite artist and song in the middle
- Add the label design to your 'Positive Patchwork' (see page 96)

Music has always been a massive part of my life; making music was all I wanted to do when I was younger, it was what I specialised in at university, and it is through music that I met my husband, Tom. It has always been a way for me to express myself creatively – until I discovered crafting and embroidery too. I don't play music as much as I used to, but I do love listening to and discovering new music.

The label on this 7" is inspired by my brother-in-law, who has a real passion for dance music. He recently left his long-term job to make a complete career change but dance music remains his creative outlet. I think it's amazing how he has taken on the challenge. It can be a really scary thing to leave something you've done for years and start something new but don't be afraid to take a big step in your career or another aspect of your life – if it's going to make you happy I think you should just go for it!

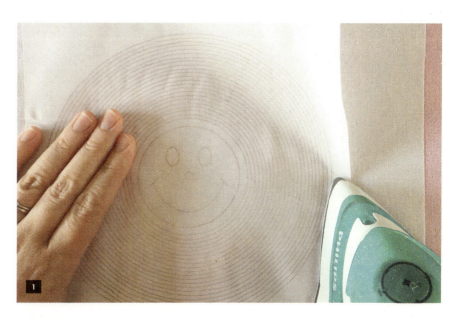

INSTRUCTIONS

1. Transfer the design onto the fabric using a permanent method of transfer. Take your time with this bit – it will be worth it to get all those circles nice and even!

2. Place the fabric in the 8" embroidery hoop and tighten it. Using 6 strands of black thread, stitch around the outer circle in small backstitches, keeping your stitches as even as you can.

3. Repeat this with the next 3 circles on the outer edge, before transferring the fabric into your 7" embroidery hoop. Make sure you are happy with the position of the outer circle in the hoop before tightening it. Then stitch the remaining circles except the inside one that will be the edge of the label. The tiny one at the very centre of the design should be stitched in black too.

4. Now using 3 strands of black thread, stitch the eyes

in satin stitch. Then stitch the mouth with 6 strands of thread using small backstitches.

5. Thread a needle with 3 strands of yellow thread. Stitch using horizontal satin stitch around the eyes and mouth to fill in the label, making sure you cover the pencil line around the edge of the circle. Stitch right up to the little circle in the middle, leaving the central circle blank to let the fabric show through.

6. Remove the fabric from the hoop and press around the edges with an iron, being careful not to iron over your stitching. Place in the embroidery hoop and tighten it, before finishing the back.

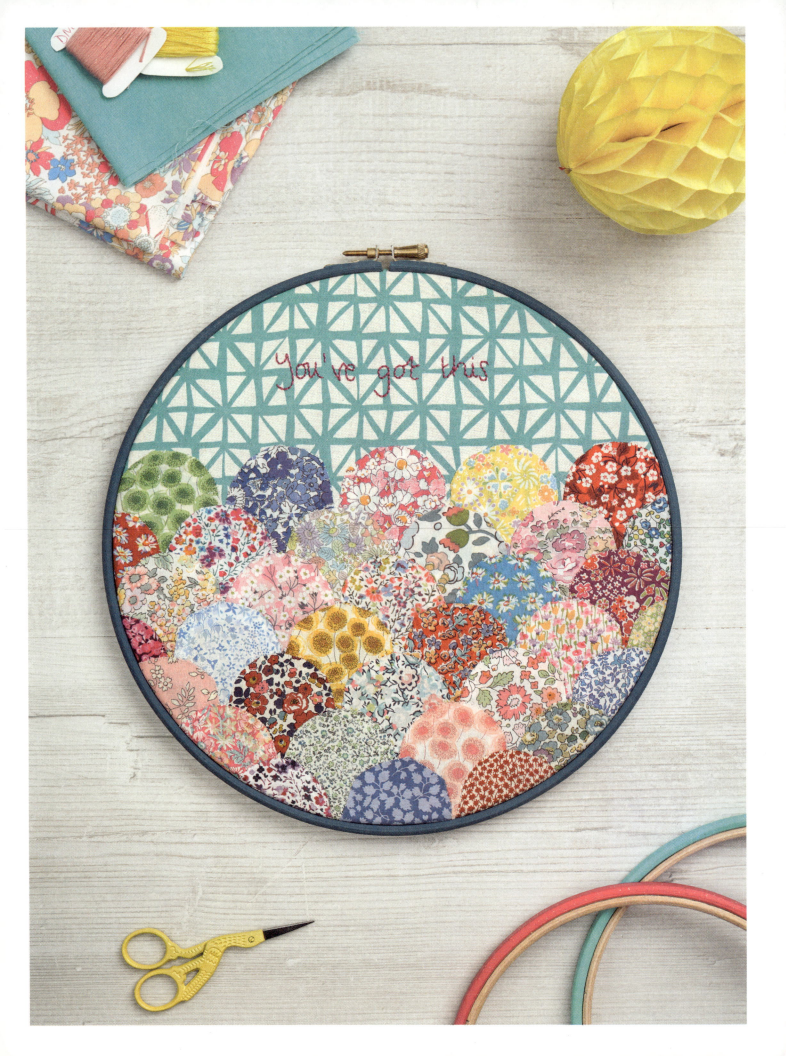

clamshell patchwork hoop

This is a project where you don't need to be an expert in another craft to make it. One of the great things about displaying the clamshells in a hoop is that once they are stitched, there is no quilting or binding necessary. Just enjoy the process!

Materials:
- 25cm (10") embroidery hoop
- Various fabrics with small prints, cut into 6x6cm (2½") squares. Find precuts on eBay
- Small piece of cardboard
- A pencil
- Sharp fabric scissors
- Some kitchen foil
- General use scissors
- An iron
- Two bits of background fabric, measuring 35x18cm (14x11") and 14x2.5cm (5x1")
- White cotton thread – I used Gütermann, shade **800**
- Air erasable pen
- A skein of embroidery thread in your chosen colour – I used shade **917**
- Water-based paint for the hoop (optional)

Make it your own:
- Use plain fabric and backstitch or running stitch 2mm from the curved edges to give a more quilted look

I have always enjoyed trying out new crafts and techniques and I have documented my crafting journey on my blog. In the spirit of experimentation, I wanted to include a skill that was new to me in this book. I love quilting, but it really isn't my thing; mainly because I usually work by eye, so all the measuring and neat cutting out puts my head in a spin! But I have always wanted to give clamshell patchwork a go, so this seemed like the perfect opportunity.

I have used a selection of Liberty prints for the clamshells in this hoop. Liberty designs are perfect for small patchwork projects because of the small designs on the fabrics. You can easily pick up pre-cut charm packs on eBay, which save a lot of time in terms of preparation. If, like me, you are not keen on measuring, they are really useful! I chose some funky background fabric that really contrasted with the Liberty prints, which I think makes all the patterns stand out beautifully in this hoop. The quote is handwritten with an air erasable pen because I wanted it to feel like a 'note to self' – a little personal positive reminder – but you could use any phrase you like.

INSTRUCTIONS

1. Choose which fabrics you want to use for the clamshells and press them to remove any creases. Cut your fabric into squares beforehand if you are not using pre-cut fabric.

2. Trace the clamshell template onto a piece of card and carefully cut it out. You might find it helpful to do a spare one in case the original one gets torn. Then, using a sharp pencil, trace around the template on the reverse of one of your fabric squares. You'll need to make sure that the template is in the very centre of the square as the seam allowance is quite tight. If you are less worried about wasting fabric, just use slightly bigger squares.

3. Draw around the template on the remaining fabric squares, making sure you check you are tracing the clamshell on the reverse of each piece of fabric. For this hoop I made 36 clamshells (plus 2 spares just in case!).

4. Cut round each clamshell shape, leaving about 1 cm (just under ½") around the edge.
The 2½" squares leave just enough room for this.

5. Cut a square piece of kitchen foil a little larger than your clamshells, making sure you use general purpose scissors and not your fabric ones. Place a fabric clamshell right side down on top of the foil with the card template in position on top. Then use the foil to fold the fabric over the top edge of the card template and press the foil firmly around the card.

6. Make sure that the curved edge of the foil is smooth before pressing with an iron, foil side up. I used a fairly hot iron with a little steam, and I ironed both sides to make sure that they were firmly pressed. Remove the foil to reveal a curved, pressed edge. Repeat with the other clamshells.

7. Place the pressed background fabric on a flat surface and put the hoop over the top of it to work out how much of the fabric you want showing in your design. Lay out the top line of clamshells. I used 5, working from the centre outwards. They should be level, with the bottoms of each curved edge next to each other but not touching. Pin in place. At this point, you may wish to work out the layout of all of the clamshells in the whole design or you can just build it up as you go. The rows should be laid out as follows:

Top row = 5 clamshells

Row 2 = 6 clamshells

Row 3 = 7 clamshells

Row 4 = 6 clamshells

Row 5 = 5 clamshells

Row 6 = 4 clamshells

Row 7 = 3 clamshells

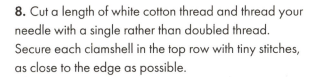

8. Cut a length of white cotton thread and thread your needle with a single rather than doubled thread. Secure each clamshell in the top row with tiny stitches, as close to the edge as possible.

9. Position the clamshells on the second row, with the bottom of each curved edge meeting the flat edges of the shells above. Check that you are happy with the position, pin them in place and then stitch them together. Repeat with the remaining rows of clamshells.

10. Pin the small piece of background fabric to the bottom 3 clamshells, so it protrudes about 1cm from the bottom. Stitch with a small running stitch along the flat bottom edge. Add a couple of small stitches on the corner of each of the 3 clamshells to secure too.

11. Press the fabric on the reverse, taking care over the clamshells to make sure that the seams are flat. Then place in your hoop, making sure that the middle shell in

the top row is in the centre, and that the two outer shells in the top row are right on the edge of the hoop. Adjust as required, leaving enough fabric around the edge of the hoop to be able to finish the back of the hoop when you have finished. Tighten the hoop to secure the fabric in position.

12. With an air erasable pen, write your quote on the background fabric. You may find that it disappears a little as you stitch, so just write over it again if you need to.

13. Thread your needle with 3 strands of embroidery thread, and stitch over the letters with a small backstitch. Where letters are not joined, tie off at the end so the thread won't show through the fabric at the front of the hoop.

14. Make sure the fabric is nice and tight in the hoop (undo it and readjust if not) and then trim the edges of the fabric to around 2.5cm (1") before finishing the back.

one step at a time geometric hoop

This is one of my favourite ways to use satin stitch (other than the ombré effect used in my 'Keep Your Hopes Up' hoop). Seeing the design take shape as you stitch more geometric blocks is really fun! Don't be afraid to make it your own.

Materials:

- 20x20cm (8x8") white linen fabric

- 10cm (4") embroidery hoop, plus a 12.5cm (5") or 15cm (6") hoop for stitching the design in

- Plenty of embroidery thread – I used 1 skein of the following colours:
  Red: **666, 321, 498**
  Orange: **970, 946, 920**
  Peach: **20, 3341, 3340**
  Yellow: **973, 728, 783**
  Green: **16, 704, 702**
  Mint: **955, 913, 911**
  Aqua: **964, 959, 3812**
  Blue: **3845, 3843, 3842**
  Lavender: **3840, 3839, 3838**
  Purple: **210, 208, 3837**
  Fuchsia: **3609, 3607, 917**
  Pink: **605, 603, 601**
  The text colour is **311**

- 20cm piece of ribbon

- Water-based paint for the hoop (optional)

Make it your own:

- Experiment with colours – this design would look great with just 3 colours

- Use a patterned fabric or plain colour linen instead

In addition to colour, pattern plays a big part in my work and I love browsing through books or Pinterest to find different designs. Geometric patterns have always appealed to me because I just find them so pleasing! Stitching them takes time, but I really enjoy stitching this design in particular. The pattern was something that I originally stitched for a campaign for the small business community, Indie Roller. I had the pleasure of speaking to Leona (who runs Indie Roller) at the blogger event Blogtacular in 2018. She's just so passionate about supporting small businesses and I felt super inspired after our conversation (so thanks, Leona!). If you haven't heard about Indie Roller, there's a link in the back of this book – you should definitely check it out.

This project uses mainly satin stitch, and I would highly recommend using a thread conditioner as it will improve the overall look of the hoop. There are a lot of colours listed here for such a small project, but I love the effect of the 3D block. Just use fewer colours in a more limited colour palette if you prefer – this is a perfect design to experiment with!

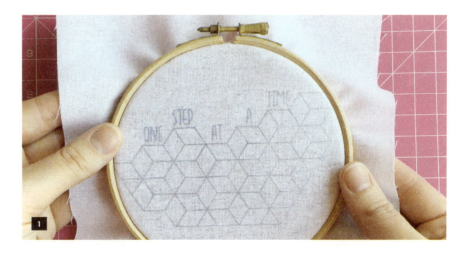

INSTRUCTIONS

1. Transfer the design onto the fabric and place in a larger hoop. This design will just fit in a 5" hoop for stitching but you'll need to move your stitching around a bit to stitch the outer squares so you might prefer to use a 6" hoop.

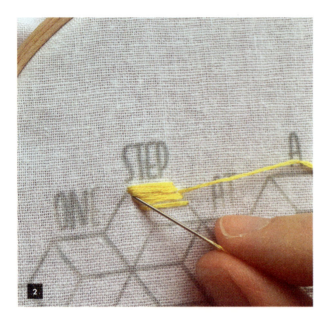

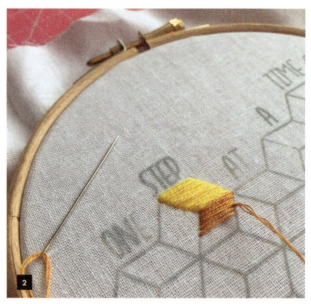

2. Thread a needle with 3 strands of the first colour you want to use – pick the lightest shade to start with. Then, starting with the top block under the word 'step' stitch the top diamond shape using a horizontal satin stitch. When you have completed this first block, thread your needle with 3 strands of the darkest shade of the same colour and stitch the diamond shape underneath in the same direction.

3. The middle shade of each colour should then be stitched diagonally, to achieve the sense of stacked 3D blocks. Stitch with 3 strands of thread making sure that there are no gaps where the 3 colours meet.

4. Repeat the stitching on the remaining blocks until complete. I didn't plan the colours beforehand but just chose them as I went along, making sure the colours worked well together.

5. To stitch the text, thread a needle with 2 strands of thread, and stitch using small backstitches over the letters. Tie off the thread at the end of each word. The letters are small enough and close enough together that you don't need to do this at the end of each letter.

6. Finish the back of your hoop, and then tie a ribbon to the top of the hoop so that it is ready to display.

positive patchwork

The hand embroidery in this project uses just a simple backstitch for the text, but you could be more adventurous with the patchwork design if you like. The text has an extra personal touch when it is handwritten, which works well for this project.

Materials:
- A 45x80cm (18x31") piece of both outer and lining fabrics – I used Liberty fabric from Alice Caroline and Kona cotton for the lining in cerise **1066** – see suppliers on page 134 for details
- Sewing machine
- Standard cotton thread – I used Gütermann **733**
- An iron
- Sharp scissors
- Pinking shears
- 2 strips of each fabric measuring 40x4.5cm (16x2")
- White linen fabric scraps
- Air erasable pen
- A 15cm (6") embroidery hoop for stitching in
- DMC embroidery thread:
  3821 gold
  917 magenta
  943 green
  plus white perlé

Make it your own:
- Make a cushion or add some 'Easy Peasy Patches', see page 74

When it comes to crafting, there are so many ways of adapting a particular technique or skill so that it works for you. If, like me, you love patchwork but just can't get to grips with it, there are plenty of beautiful pre-printed patchwork fabrics for you to choose instead (like the one I have used for this project). But equally, if you love patchwork, you could easily create your own for this project too. Experimentation is something that I am passionate about when it comes to crafting, but it is sometimes equally important to recognise your weaknesses and adapt techniques to suit you too.

I couldn't resist this beautiful Liberty fabric for my positive patchwork. It includes some of my favourite prints in the most gorgeous colours and I knew it would be wonderful to work with. This project is a long-term project because you can keep adding to it over a period of time. I chose to make it into a project bag because they are so handy.

INSTRUCTIONS
1. To make the bag, iron both pieces of fabric and lay them out flat with the outer fabric facing upwards on top. Pin together, ensuring that there are no creases – I put a pin in the centre of each patchwork square.

2. Stitch along the lines of the patchwork print with your sewing machine. Take your time to ensure that you are following the lines carefully. Trim any loose thread at the edges.

3. Press the fabric. Turn over 2cm on one of the shorter ends and press, before turning half of this under and pressing again to create the top edge of the bag. Repeat with the other shorter end and then stitch each short end on your machine, 1cm from the folded edge.

4. Fold the fabric in half with outer sides together, lining up the top edges very carefully. Pin the side edges and stitch together on your machine, 2cm from the edge. Trim the seams to 1cm with pinking shears, and cut the bottom corners diagonally to prevent fraying.

5. To make the handles, take one strip of both fabrics and place one on top of the other with right sides together. Pin down the middle, then stitch around the edges 1cm from the edge, leaving a gap of 5-6cm for turning out.

6. Trim the seams to 0.5cm, clipping the corners diagonally, before turning right side out. Press with the iron, ensuring the edges are folded inside the gap. Close the gap with a slip stitch or small running stitch.

7. Position the handles on the bag, pin and stitch them in place on your machine. Stitch a rectangle to secure them to the bag and then stitch two diagonal lines across the rectangle for extra strength.

8. Place a piece of ironed white linen in the embroidery hoop. Write out your chosen quotes on the linen using an air erasable pen. Stitch over the text using small backstitches.

9. Remove the fabric from the hoop and cut out a rectangle around the quotes. Position on your bag and then pin in place, before stitching with white perlé (or 3 strands of white embroidery thread) in backstitch around the edges of the fabric.

take time out to be creative hoop

This project combines both a pattern and some freehand stitching, so it's good to start with if you want to bring a little more freedom into your work. Let your creativity really flow with this hoop!

Materials:

- 27x27cm (roughly 11x11") piece of fabric
- 18cm (7") embroidery hoop
- DMC embroidery thread:
  349 red
  3340 orange
  17 yellow
  16 green
  958 teal
  800 pale blue
  792 dark blue
  553 purple
  3708 pink
  995 bright blue for the handwritten text
- Permanent method of design transfer
- Water-based paint for the hoop (optional)

Make it your own:

- Use a smaller colour palette, or even one single colour for the word 'creative'
- Use a plain fabric for the background instead of a patterned one
- Stitch a banner instead of a hoop

There are lots of different quotes in the projects in this book, but if I had to choose one to sum up the main idea of my book then "take time out to be creative" would be it. A few years ago, my friend Daria and I set out to start a joint creative project, and this was our strap line to sum up our idea. We both felt very strongly that creativity needs space to be nurtured and developed and we both used the creative time outside our day jobs as a way of improving our overall wellbeing. Daria is still my partner in craft, and I'm really grateful to her for her friendship and support.

This hoop uses negative space embroidery, which has become really popular recently. It's no wonder really because it's fun to stitch and the finished effect is fantastic. This project requires a little freehand stitching and design as you go along, but it means that every piece will be unique. As I've mentioned before, don't be put off by this but embrace it and enjoy stitching using a different technique.

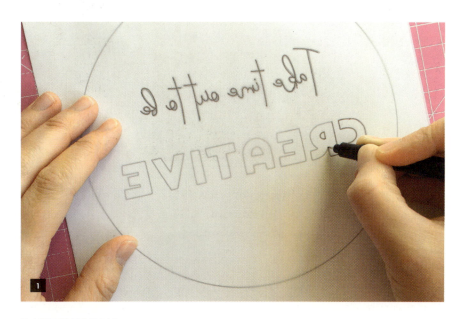

INSTRUCTIONS

1. Transfer the design onto your fabric and place in the embroidery hoop.

2. Thread your needle with 3 strands of shade 995, and use small backstitches to stitch the words 'take time out to be'. (You may wish to consult the hand lettering tips on page 12).

3. The word 'creative' is stitched more freely, using straight stitches. It's entirely up to you where you position the colours, how much of each one you use in each colour block and the direction of the stitches.

Continue to use 3 strands of thread for this part of the hoop. Always work from the letter edge outwards, making sure that the stitches around the letters cover the lines of the letters to give the effect of negative space. Work the straight stitches in satin stitch, leaving gaps in between the stitches. Fill in the gaps with more stitches. Remember to spread out the colours so that it looks like a real colour splash!

Once you have completed the stitching, check for any gaps that you might have missed and then fill in as needed. Paint your hoop if you wish, before finishing the back of your hoop

quilting hoop clock

Quilting hoops are brilliant for larger projects, because their depth (usually around 2cm) gives scope for using them in a different way. Here, it allows for the clock mechanism to be hidden at the back.

Materials:
- 41x41cm (16x16")
  piece of white felt
- 41x41cm (16x16")
  piece of white cotton
  fabric
- Felt: 1 sheet of 20x30cm
  (8x12") 1mm thick felt in
  Neon Pink, Mr Happy,
  Mermaid, Aegean,
  Bonbon and gold glitter
- Threads to match felt:
  **E1010, 444, 943,
  3844, 604, 3822**
- 30cm (12") quilting
  hoop
- Paper scissors
- Sharp fabric scissors
- An iron
- A few pins
- A piece of card bigger
  than the hoop (or two
  bits to stick together will
  be fine)
- A pen and pencil
- Water-based paint for
  the hoop (optional)
- Clock mechanism
- Ruler or tape measure
- A craft knife or scalpel
- Cutting mat

In the spirit of taking time out to be creative, I thought it would be fun to include a project for a hoop clock. This is something I have never done before, but I thought that it was about time that I had one for my craft room! Lots of the hoop clocks I have seen on Pinterest are quite small, so I decided to go super-size and use a 12" quilting hoop for this project. You need to use a quilting hoop rather than an embroidery hoop for this make, as the depth of the quilting hoops allow for the clock mechanism to be inserted at the back.

I have used some beautiful wool felt from Cloud Craft for this project (see list of suppliers on page 134) in a bright, modern colour palette. I think the glitter felt is amazing, so used some of that too. The exact shades are given in the materials list opposite but you could always use acrylic felt, which is readily available on the high street, instead if you prefer.

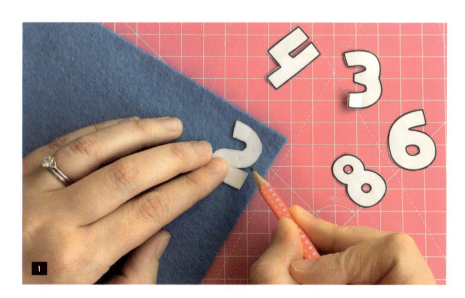

INSTRUCTIONS
1. Work out which colour felt you want to use for each number. Cut out the paper templates (not with your fabric scissors!) and place them right side down on the felt. Draw around each one with a pencil, and then carefully cut out each number with your fabric scissors.

2. Iron the large piece of felt on a very low heat to remove any creases. Position the numbers on the felt (using the quilting hoop and clock hands as a guide), and then pin them in place.

3. Stitch each number onto the felt with 3 strands of matching thread using small backstitches. I added a little more texture to each number by stitching 2 further lines inside the outer one.

4. Take out the inner hoop from the quilting hoop and trace around the outside of it with pencil on a piece of card. Paint your hoop at this point if you wish, leaving to dry before moving on to the next step.

5. Position the felt in the hoop with the white fabric underneath it, making sure that the felt is centred and that you are happy with the tension of the fabrics. Take the clock hands and position them in the middle of the clock, using a ruler or tape measure to help. Mark the middle of the hands with a small dot – I used a pencil first and then marked it with pen once the hands were removed, just to make sure that the mark was permanent.

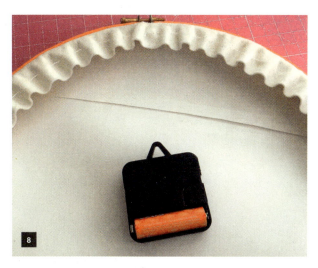

6. You may want someone to help with the next step. Place your hoop on a cutting mat. Using a craft knife or scalpel, cut a very small cross over the dot that you made in the middle of the hoop. Take your time over this stage as you don't want to make too big a hole. Make sure you cut through the felt and the white fabric. Place the card in the back of the hoop, mark the centre, and then cut a hole in the card in the same way as the fabric - making sure they line up.

7. Ask your helper to hold the hoop, and then push the clock mechanism through the hole in the back. Adjust the size of the hole if you need to, remembering to take your time and cut only very small amounts at a time. When you're happy, screw the nut on the front of the clock to secure and position the hands.

8. Trim the white fabric at the back of the hoop by eye to 1cm and the felt to 2.5cm. Finish the back just as the others are finished in this book (see page 13 for a guide to finishing your hoops).

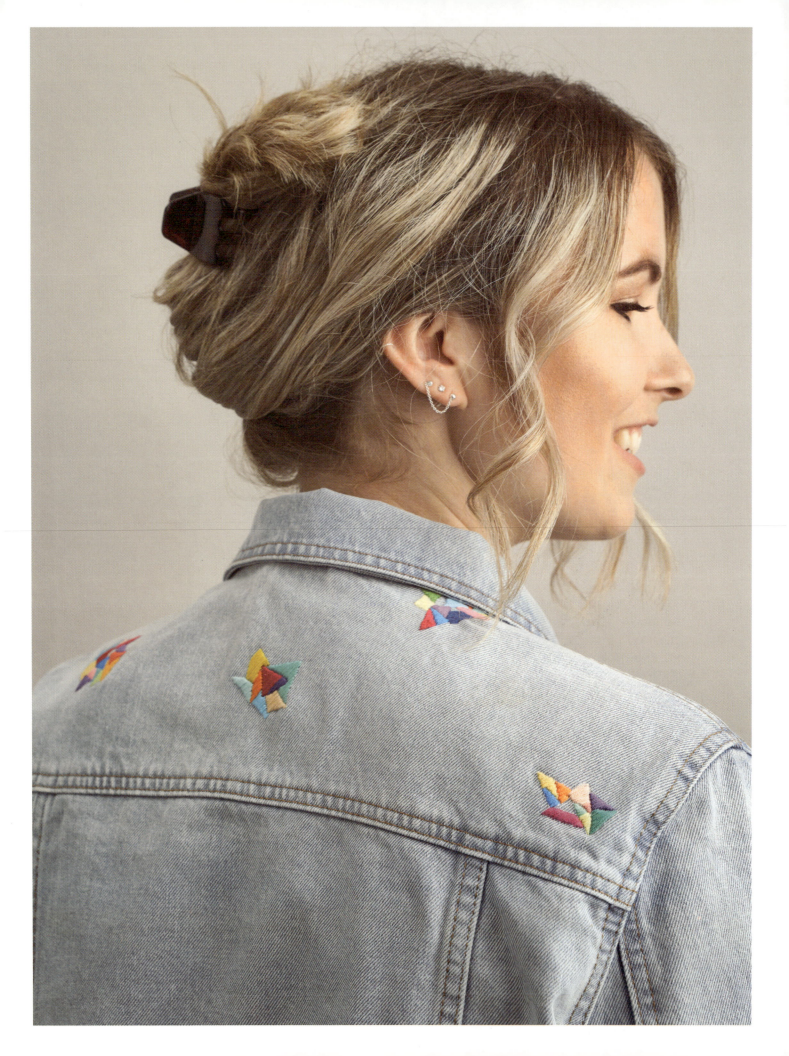

customised denim jacket

Denim can be quite tough to stitch on, so washing it beforehand can help to soften it. Use a sharp needle to stitch and the weave of the fabric to guide your stitching. Draw small sections at a time, and enjoy the slow process of this project.

Materials:
- A denim jacket
- Lightweight interfacing, big enough to cover the back shoulder panel of the jacket
- Loose ends of thread (or a selection of your own specific colours)
- An air erasable pen
- An iron

Make it your own:
- Stitch a different panel on the jacket
- Design something with doodles instead – flowers, little characters, a combination of lots of different designs would work well
- Stitch a backpack or another garment instead!

This is a really long-term project that is lovely to work on as and when you fancy doing it. A customised denim jacket is a work in progress that will develop over time. There is absolutely no rush to finish it and it doesn't actually matter if it never gets finished! Sewing your jacket in small sections means that it will look good enough to wear at any stage of the project.

I have chosen to customise this jacket using loose ends of threads from other projects, so the colours are chosen at random. I love the freedom of this type of project but, as with the previous loose ends projects, do feel free to choose your own specific colour palette if you prefer. However you choose to stitch this denim jacket it will be unique; we will all have our own unique jackets to wear!

INSTRUCTIONS

1. Wash, dry and iron your jacket. Then turn it inside out, and cut a piece of lightweight interfacing big enough to cover the back shoulder panel (I just did this by eye). Iron it onto the inside of the jacket, according to manufacturer's instructions.

2. Turn the jacket the right way out and lay it on a flat surface. Use the air erasable pen to draw the first shape. I drew a small triangle to start. Thread a needle with 3 strands of a colour from your loose ends, and then cover the shape with satin stitch. Don't worry if you run out of a particular colour half way through stitching a shape – just use another colour as I have done here.

3. Draw a few more shapes around the first one, and then continue to stitch with different colours to build up your design. You could even leave a few shapes unstitched in the middle so that the denim shows through in some places.

4. Although the design and stitching process for this jacket is very free, you might want to think about these tips to help:
■ Keep the size of the shapes quite small, as this will help to maintain the right tension of thread as you stitch. If it is too loose, it will just look baggy rather than being neat and tidy.

- Don't draw too many shapes in advance or the pen marks will disappear. Stick to drawing one or two at a time, drawing over the lines again as you need to.

- As you stitch, don't leave big gaps between stitches in case you run out of the colour thread you are using. Complete a smaller colour block and switch to another colour if the shape is not covered.

- Using a thread conditioner will really help the stitching process and will also help to maintain the look of the stitching as you wear the jacket.

- I decided to stitch a few small areas over the back shoulder panel on my jacket, which I will build up as I continue to work on my design. I haven't decided whether or not to join them all up yet – that's a decision I will make later. You could stitch one large area, working from one side of the jacket if you prefer – the beauty of this project is that you can do whatever works for you. Enjoy the freedom of the project and the time that you take to stitch it!

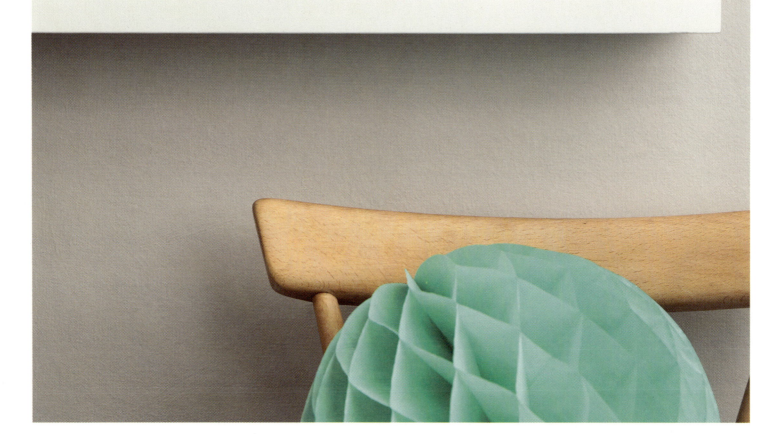

framed alphabet embroidery

This heirloom project looks wonderful on display in a child's bedroom, and is designed to fit easily in a standard (9x9") frame. It takes time to stitch, so it is something that you'll keep coming back to – but once complete you'll love it!

Materials:

- 27x27cm (11x11") piece of white linen fabric
- A permanent method of transferring the design onto the fabric
- A 20cm (8") hoop
- DMC embroidery thread:
  666 red
  947 orange
  972 gold
  307 yellow
  16 green
  958 teal
  996 light blue
  824 dark blue
  333 purple
  603 light pink
  601 dark pink
- Sharp fabric scissors
- A picture frame - I used a 23x23cm / 9x9" white Ribba frame from Ikea
- Scotch tape
- Scissors

Make it your own:
- Design your own background – trace the grid and letters and then draw your own patterns

At the time of writing this book, Little One is at the point of already knowing her alphabet and she is getting into spelling things. "How do you spell...?" is a very common phrase in our house, and it's amazing to see how a child learns and develops vocabulary. She's making connections between words that start with the same letter, and absolutely loves to spell her name. It has been tricky juggling book writing with family life and work, but Tom has made it possible for me to do it and I will be forever grateful to him for his love and support. This project is for them, and Little One told me that she loves it, which made me very happy.

This project only uses satin stitch, so it is quite time consuming but worth it for the overall effect. I used a select colour palette of 11 colours, but you could use fewer or more colours as you prefer. It's a lovely project to keep coming back to and stitching a bit more when you feel like it.

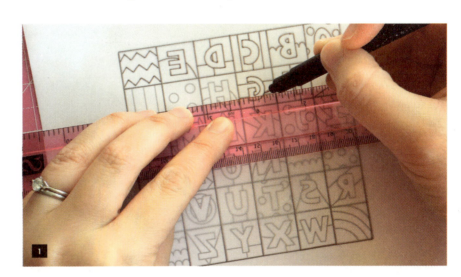

INSTRUCTIONS

1. Transfer the design onto the fabric using a permanent method, as this project takes a while to stitch; you don't want it to disappear! Transferring the design does take a little time to complete, so don't rush it. Place the fabric in your embroidery hoop and secure in place.

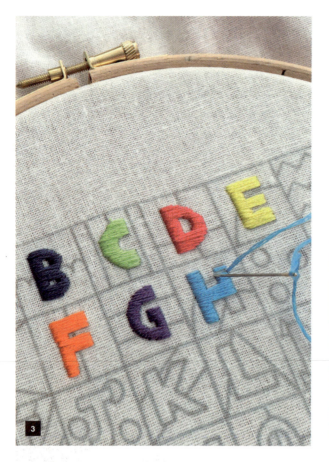

2. This project is stitched entirely in satin stitch, so here are some tips for sewing:

■ Always use 3 strands of embroidery thread and thread conditioner.

■ Start by stitching the letters first and then go back and fill in the background. Make sure you stitch all the letters with horizontal stitches so it looks neat.

■ When stitching the background for each square, try to alternate the direction of the stitches. I started horizontally for the letter 'A' then vertically for 'B'. On the row below, I stitched the square under 'A' vertically, and so on.

■ Keep your thread organised as you stitch by using a labelled thread organiser or a piece of card. This will really help when you keep coming back to this project.

3. When all the design is complete, remove from the hoop. Trim the fabric around the edge of the design – cut a square of about 2.5cm (1") around the edge of your stitching.

4. Take the mount out of the frame and place it on top of the stitching. When you are happy with the position, stick the fabric in place with some Scotch tape at the back of the mount (the Scotch tape can be easily removed if the positioning needs to be adjusted). Place the mount back in the frame and secure the back so that it is ready to hang.

embroidery materials

Quilting cottons are perfect for embroidery projects and you'll find a fat quarter goes a long way

Scissors come in various shapes and sizes, so find a pair that feels comfortable to you

ESSENTIALS

Below you will find a list of the materials and tools I could not do without when I am working on a project:

Embroidery hoops – I use Elbessee hoops because I love the quality of them. The quilting hoop you will need for the clock on page 104 is also made by Elbessee.

Fabric – Essex linen is a firm favourite of mine because it's so lovely to stitch on. The weave allows you to see where you're stitching, so it is especially good for satin stitch. I also stitch on quilting cotton, which comes in lots of colours and designs so it's perfect for making a project unique.

Thread – I always use DMC thread for my projects. The colour codes for all the different types of DMC thread are the same, so if you choose the same colour code in standard embroidery thread or perlé, for example, you can be sure they are the same colour.

Needles – the type of needles you use are a matter of preference. I have quite big hands so I prefer to use Prym sharps in size 7 or 5. If you're new to embroidery, buy a pack of mixed size sharps (widely available from different brands) and try out the different sized needles until you find one you feel happy with.

Thread conditioner – this technically could be on the 'useful but not essential' list, but I personally can't stitch without it! I used to use 'Thread Heaven', but the company has recently stopped producing this so you may not be able to find it. 'Thread Magic' is a similar alternative and you can find that easily on eBay. Both of these conditioners are man-made so are also suitable if you are a vegan stitcher.

Scissors – I would recommend investing in a few decent pairs of scissors, as they can make all the difference to your projects. Use a small pair of sharps for general work, and a larger pair for cutting. My preferred brand is Fiskars, but scissors are widely available from other brands.

This vellum paper requires that you transfer your designs in reverse and then iron them onto the fabric

I love to paint my hoops and have a large selection of tester pots in different colours to use for this

Transfer pen – I use the very fine pens from Sublime Stitching as they are so lovely to use. Other pens can be a bit too thick for fine, detailed work and I always prefer to transfer designs permanently. Air erasable pens are also very handy, and they are easy to find on eBay.

A screwdriver – not what immediately comes to mind when you think about embroidery! However, screwdrivers are really handy for tightening the screw at the top of the embroidery hoop when your project is finished. Using a screwdriver makes sure that your hoop is tightened securely.

USEFUL BUT NOT ESSENTIAL
There are some other materials and tools that aren't essential, but you may find useful:

Scissor sharpener – particularly useful tool for when you are cutting felt, which blunts scissors easily. I have the Fiskars sharpener and it was a really great long-term investment.

Vellum paper – if you decide to try out the Sublime Stitching pens, you'll need to use them with 100gsm translucent vellum. You trace the design in reverse and then iron it on with a very cool iron with no steam. Practise on some scrap fabric pieces beforehand to test it out.

DMC Magic Paper – brilliant for transferring designs onto stretchy fabrics such as jersey. It is widely available with pre-printed designs or as plain sheets.

Rotary cutter – really useful for cutting out pieces of fabric. You'll also need a cutting mat to protect the surface you are cutting on.

Water-based paint – one of my trademarks is to paint the embroidery hoops I use to display my work. I love adding an extra pop of colour to a project by painting the hoop in a contrasting colour. If you prefer the natural look, you can always leave them unpainted.

embroidery stitch guide

This is a step-by-step guide to the basic embroidery stitches used in this book. If you are just starting out, use a test hoop to practise the stitches before you start the projects

STRAIGHT STITCH

1. Bring your needle up through the fabric at the start of the stitch.

2. Insert the needle back through the fabric at the desired length.

BACKSTITCH

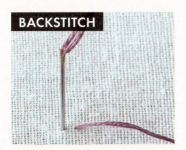

1. Insert the needle through the back of the fabric to start the stitch. Work out the size of the stitch.

2. Pull the thread through the fabric to make your first stitch.

3. To one side, bring the needle up through the fabric to make another stitch the same size.

4. Push the needle through the fabric where your first stitch ended, so they meet. Pull the thread through to make your second stitch.

5. You should now have two stitches the same size.

6. Repeat, keeping each stitch similar in length. Make sure the stitches are touching end to end.

SATIN STITCH

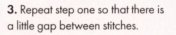

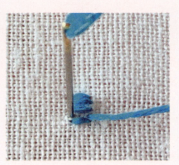

1. Bring your needle up through the fabric and position it based on how long the stitch needs to be (using the pattern or lines you have drawn as a guide).

2. Pull the thread through the fabric to make your first stitch.

3. Repeat step one so that there is a little gap between stitches.

4. Pull the thread through the fabric to make your second stitch.

5. Fill in the gaps with more stitches, but don't leave big gaps.

FRENCH KNOTS

1. Insert the needle through the back of the fabric where the knot needs to be. Pull the thread taut.

2. Place the needle in front of the thread, and then wrap the thread over the needle towards you.

3. Wrap the thread around the needle twice to make a medium-sized knot and three times to make a bigger knot.

4. With the needle in front of the thread, place it back through the fabric next to where it originally came up.

5. Push the knot down to the bottom of the needle and hold it tight with your thumb.

6. Pull the thread through the fabric until a knot is formed. Tie a knot at the back to finish. Don't pull too hard or the knot will lose shape or come through the fabric.

TEMPLATE INFORMATION

All templates included here are full size. Patterns for hoops include a circle indicating placement, but the circle itself should not be transferred onto fabric. The only exception is the Long Player Hoop on Page 84, which is slightly bigger than a 7" hoop so the design goes right to the edge.

Good Vibes Hoop Page 16

Heart Felt Brooch
Page 20

**Speech Bubble
Pincushion**
Page 28

**Rainbow Mini
Hoop Necklace**
Page 24

Happy Clothes Labels Page 32

YOU LOOK LOVELY TODAY

15mm x 80mm (finished length = 60mm)

YAY FOR TODAY!

25mm x 80mm (finished length = 60mm)

**Live Colourfully
Hoop** Page 36

Happy Clothes Labels Page 32

YES YOU CAN

20mm x 60mm (cut double so finished length = 60mm and actual length of ribbon is 120mm)

Yay Mini Hoop Page 40

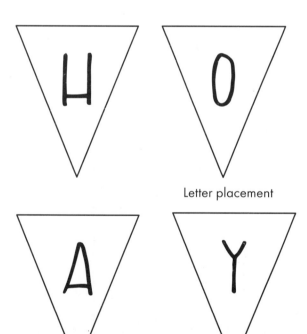

Letter placement

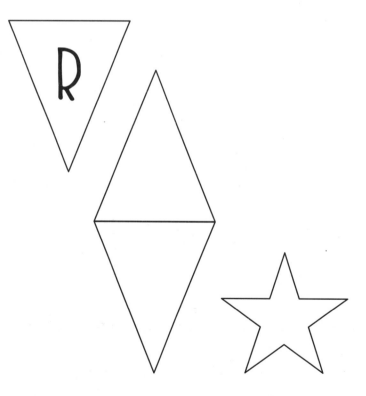

Bunting Cake Topper Page 44

Cut one for each of the letters H, R, A and Y.
Cut out two for letter O

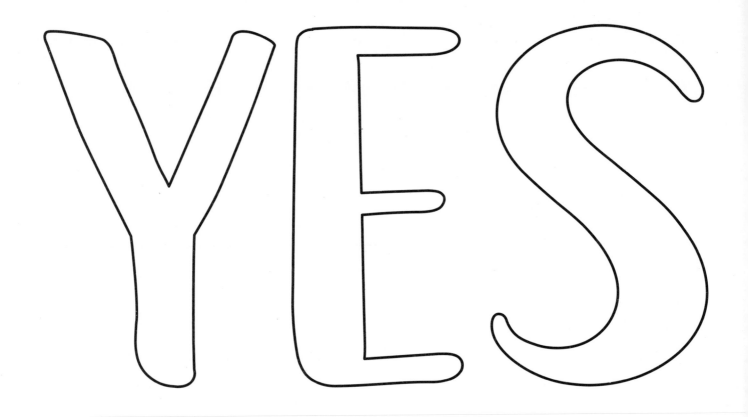

Yes You Can Banner Page 50

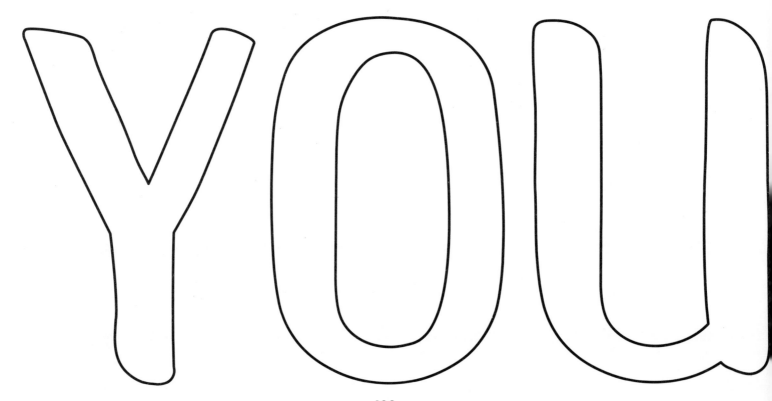

Yes You Can Banner Page 50

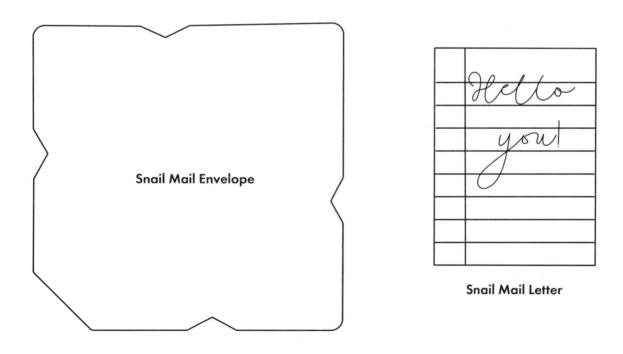

Snail Mail Envelope

Snail Mail Letter

Snail Mail Hoop Page 58

Cut x2

Cut x3

Diagram to show placement

Blue Skies Hoop

Page 54

today's
the day!

Double-sided banner
Page 62

125

Not today

Double-sided banner
Page 62

Keep Your Hopes Up Hoop Page 70

**Easy Peasy
Patches**
Page 74

**Naptime Crafter
Sweatshirt**
Page 78

Long Player 7" hoop Page 84

Clamshell Patchwork Hoop
Page 88

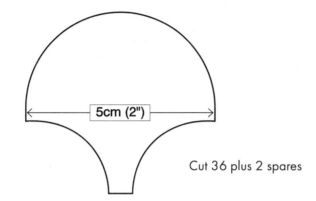

Cut 36 plus 2 spares

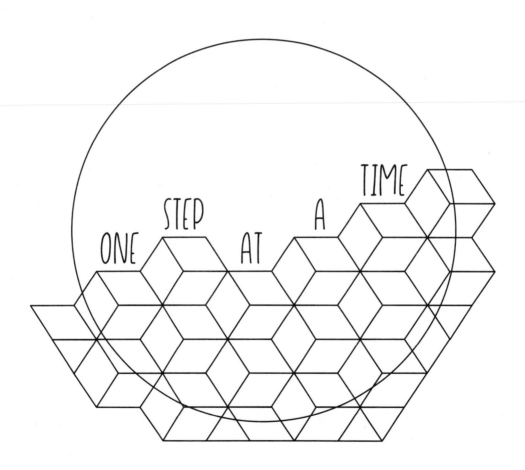

One Step at a Time Geometric Hoop Page 92

Take Time Out to be Creative Hoop Page 100

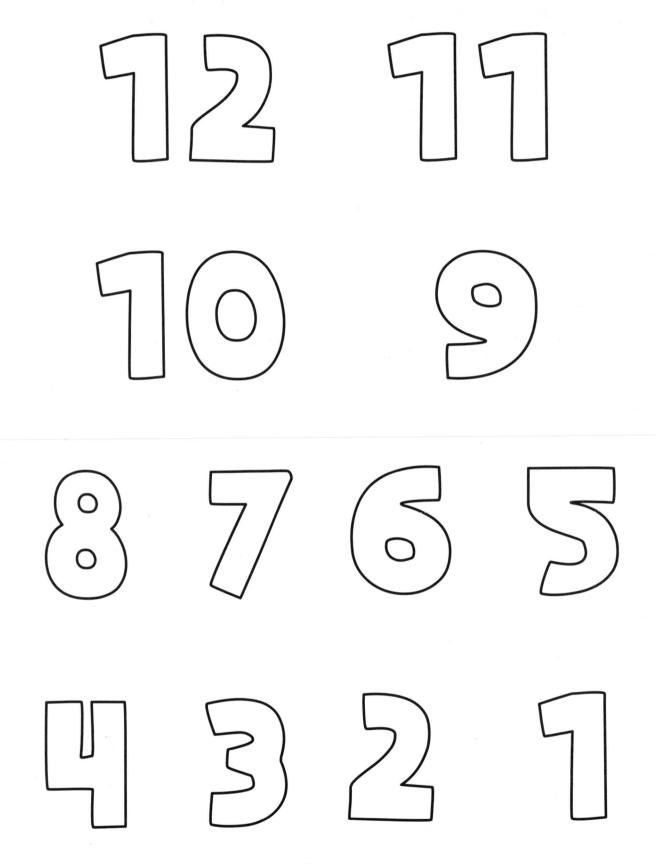

Quilting Hoop Clock Page 104

Framed Alphabet Embroidery Page 112

craft suppliers

Cloud Craft A fantastic selection of wool felt sheets, DMC thread, hoops and other tools. *www.cloudcraft.co.uk*

Craft Felt Perfect for acrylic felt for vegan crafters. There is a good selection of colours and I have always been pleased with the quality. *www.craftfelt.co.uk*

The Fabric Fox Lots of modern, colourful and funky fabrics as well as haberdashery items. *www.thefabricfox.co.uk*

Plush Addict A very large selection of fabrics, plus they stock all shades of Kona cotton. *www.plushaddict.co.uk*

eBay Perfect for all kinds of things! I buy pom pom trim, ribbons, jewellery, accessories and thread conditioner. 'On Liberty Street' specialises in pre-cut Liberty charm squares. *www.ebay.co.uk*

Stitcher Best for DMC embroidery thread! *www.stitcher.co.uk*

Cookson Gold An excellent selection of jewellery making supplies. A bit pricier than some, but the quality is always good. *www.cooksongold.com*

Alice Caroline For the best selection of Liberty fabrics. The patchwork fabric I used for my 'Positive Patchwork' project is an exclusive design from Alice Caroline. *www.alicecaroline.com*

Cloth & Candy A wonderful selection of modern prints and haberdashery items. *www.clothandcandy.co.uk*

Hobbycraft You can usually find most things you need here, particularly haberdashery items. *www.hobbycraft.co.uk*

John Lewis haberdashery A selection is available online, but it's nice to go in and browse! They stock a good selection of fabrics, DMC thread and haberdashery items, and the plain sheets of DMC Magic Paper. *www.johnlewis.com*

Wilko A good range of paint is available in tester pots, and their paint is vegan friendly. *www.wilko.com*

B&Q An excellent selection of paint is available in tester pots, and they will colour match for you if you need a specific colour. Also useful for items such as wooden dowel. *www.diy.com*

useful links

Hello! Hooray! My website, where it all began. Here you can read all my blog posts, including lots of craft tutorials. On Hello! Hooray! you will find my shop, where you can buy ready-stitched hoops and banners, kits and haberdashery. You can also book my workshops. A DMC to Anchor thread colour code conversion chart is also available on my website to download and keep.
www.hellohooray.com

Hello! Hooray! Etsy shop You'll find all my pdf patterns here.
www.etsy.com/uk/shop/ hellohoorayshop

Mindful To read interesting articles about mindfulness and wellbeing.
www.mindful.org

Indie Roller An amazing community for independent business owners to support each other and learn more about running a business.
www.indieroller.com

ENDNOTES 1 Burrill, A. Make It Now! (London: Virgin Books, 2017), 58. **2** Mindful, 'What is Mindfulness?', Available from: *www.mindful.org/what-is-mindfulness/, 2014* (accessed 24th August 2018).

About the author

Clare Albans is a mama, maker and blogger living in Newcastle upon Tyne. A musician and teacher by trade, she looked for a creative outlet from her day job and discovered crafting. Making is now a huge part of her life. Clare started her blog, Hello! Hooray!, in 2012 as a place to share her craft projects as well as recipes and lifestyle content. Since becoming a mum in 2016, Clare has found a new focus and passion for embroidery, although Hello! Hooray! still features all her creative endeavours. Hello! Hooray! has been featured in publications such as Craftseller and Bibelot Magazine (by author and crafter Chloe Owens) and Clare has also appeared on BBC Radio 4's Woman's Hour. Clare runs a successful Hello! Hooray! online shop which is the go-to place for colourful and fun modern embroidery and patterns. She now stitches and teaches embroidery workshops full time.

Acknowledgements

Writing my first book has been incredibly exciting, inspiring and challenging, but I have loved every minute of doing something that I have always dreamt about. I'd like to thank a few people for all of their support during the process:

Tom, I absolutely could not have done this without you. You have always believed in me and encouraged me to keep going – I don't think I'll ever be able to thank you enough for your love and support. Thank you for giving me the time and space to be able to work on this, and a big thank you to you and Evie for being so patient with me.

Mum and Dad, thank you for your love, support and encouragement, and for always teaching me to try new things. Who knows if I would ever have discovered my love of embroidery without having that sense of curiosity that you always taught me to have. Thank you too for helping give me time to work on my book.

Helen, thank you for being the best proof-reader ever. I shall be forever grateful for your advice and for the time you gave helping me write this book. I feel so sad that you will not get to hold a copy of it in your hands, but so proud that you were a part of it. Keith, Naomi and Anthony, thank you for all of your love and encouragement too.

Tiffany, you have always been there to cheer me on and I hope you know how much I appreciate that. You are the best!

Daria, my partner in craft – never afraid to give me honest feedback, which I love about you!

Susie, you have always supported me and I am so proud of you.

Amy, internet friends are real friends – you've always had my back and I hope you know I've got yours too.

A big thank you to Katherine for believing in me and in my work, it means such a lot. Thank you for gathering a great team to create this book.

To my publisher, White Owl, and everyone there who has put up with my endless questions. Thank you for everything that you have done to bring my book to life. I will always be grateful for your belief in me.